Lost and Found

GREAT BARN FINDS & OTHER AUTOMOTIVE DISCOVERIES

©2009 Krause Publications, Inc., a subsidiary of F+W Media, Inc.

Published by

krause publications
A subsidiary of F+W Media, Inc.

700 East State Street • Iola, WI 54990-0001
715-445-2214 • 888-457-2873
www.krausebooks.com

Our toll-free number to place an order or obtain
a free catalog is (800) 258-0929.

Library of Congress Control Number: 2009939598

ISBN-13: 978-1-4402-1377-9
ISBN-10: 1-4402-1377-1

Designed by Sharon Bartsch
Edited by Brian Earnest

Printed in the United States of America

CONTENTS

By Angelo Van Bogart

THE CARS THAT DREAMS ARE MADE OF

The right questions and coincidences form the perfect find

Old cars and trucks have been found lurking in barns, lying forgotten in warehouses, hoarded in semi trailers and gathered in even less likely places. These slumbering vehicles vary as widely as the manner in which they are stored, but they all have one thing in common: They maintain a mysterious aura and, when they're found, it's exciting!

One of the most popular features to *Old Cars Weekly* is when readers share tales of vehicular discoveries with fellow readers. It's been written many times, but every collector dreams of finding a desirable, unmolested car or truck tucked away, and then negotiating its purchase. In this book, we have featured some of the staff's favorite discoveries of dream finds that have been realized.

The most exciting tales of discovery usu-

ally involve a crotchety old man, a prewar car not driven since Truman was president and a rickety old barn. Stories with these elements are included in this book, but to be considered a "Found!" car or truck in *Old Cars Weekly*, it's far less complicated. "Found!" cars and trucks featured in the publication have generally been stashed away for more than 20 years without having been driven, have avoided contact with the vast majority of the hobby and weren't simply found through a classified ad. Of course, a few interesting personalities surrounding an uncommon car hidden in a unique fashion with twists to its discovery make a story even more riveting, and this book offers all of these types of stories. And more.

Making your own discovery requires being at the right place at the right time. Get out and meet hobbyists. Be alert when you're out on a Sunday drive. Your dream find may be waiting for you.

Story by Sharon Thatcher
Photos courtesy of Mike Hendel and Barry Dosdall

A HENDEL GOES HOME

A rare, long lost Hendel makes a fascinating journey back to its home in Minnesota

Above, a 1936 newspaper article identifies this touring car as a Hendel. It also notes that the photo was taken in 1905 and was loaded with members of the Mr. and Mrs. Willilam Hendel family.

Part of a rare Hendel automobile has made its way back to the city of its origins: Red Wing, Minn. And the story of its journey makes its homecoming all the more remarkable.

The surviving Hendel was one of no more than three automobiles made by the successful wagon maker William Hendel at the turn of the 20th century. This particular car was ordered by a Minneapolis physician.

Although its whereabouts after the physician took delivery remains a mystery, more recently it was found in Ohio by a new property owner who wondered what kind of old vehicle sat outside a dilapidated old shed. With the wood of the auto long ago rotted away, the only clues came in the form of a frame, a wheel and a few miscellaneous parts.

Oh yes, and a wooden tool chest marked "Wm H Hendel." Inside, clinging on to the last shreds of the car's identity, were the tattered, nearly illegible remnants of a Hendel automobile ad from the Dec. 1, 1903, Cycle and Automobile Trade Journal. It described Hendel's new automaking venture.

An unidentified man is shown with the Hendel runabout. It was purchased by a Minneapolis physician. Parts of it were found in Ohio and have now been returned to Red Wing, Minnesota.

Seeking more information about the car, the owner made a phone call to the Goodhue County Historical Museum in Red Wing, where car collector Barry Dosdall answered the phone.

"I never answer the phone," Dosdall says of that fateful day. "I mow the lawn and run the boiler, but that day everyone was busy with something else and I answered the phone. On the other end was this guy in the military and he was calling from Turkey. And he said, 'Is there anyone who knows about cars in Red Wing? I found this car made in Red Wing and I want to document it.'"

Turns out, Dosdall knew a lot about old cars. "I've been car collect-

The quality of this picture makes it uncertain if it is an artist's rendering of the Hendel runabout or a faded photo that has been outlined, but it shows the unmistakable style of the physician's runabout now owned by Barry Dosdall.

ing since 1972," he says. "I've owned well over 1,000 cars. I have about 40 now that are noteworthy."

But oddly enough, the Hendel was a nearly forgotten piece of Red Wing history. "Even living here, we had heard of the car, but we thought it was a legend," he says. "I never heard a name attached."

Dosdall asked the caller several questions about the car. "I said it was probably a curved-dash Olds or something more common," he says. But the more he listened, the more he wondered. "It had some unmistakable things about it that were unique. It had some real odd wheels on it and some odd steering.

Blacksmiths would have some quirks, and you could identify them by their quirks, and it had those. He finally got my attention."

Although the Ohio owner was not originally interested in selling what was left of the car, over the course of several months, it seemed natural that the Hendel should return to Red Wing. About a year ago, it did. Dosdall is now the proud owner of the Hendel car parts and the accompanying toolbox.

Until very recently, Dosdall believed the car was the only Hendel ever made. In speaking with family members still in the area, he was told that William Hendel never found financing for his auto making venture in Red Wing so he moved to Minneapolis, but couldn't find financing there, either. No more capital meant no more cars.

A Hendel relative on the other side of Minnesota, however, had been conducting his own research and he had a different story to tell. Mike Hendel, of Dundee, found written evidence amid family papers of a car that pre-dated the physician's Hendel, and a third made afterwards.

"William was the head of the brothers' wagon business," he said. "They made very fancy wagons, down to logging wagons. They also made all the fire wagons for the City of Red Wing. They also owned a hotel. They were young entrepreneurs and William was the head of the clan."

Among Mike Hendel's papers are the recollections of William's son, George Peter Hendel, dated Aug. 8, 1982. In it are clues to the three autos:

"...I know that he built three cars. The first was a simple type – a wooden chassis ... four buggy type wheels and the rear axle solid and driven from a one cylinder engine. We little kids could run almost as fast, but going around the corner the outside wheel would set up a scraping loud noise – no differential.

"The second car was sort of a two seater type with two rear wheels free and chain driven...

"My father's hope was to build cars in Red Wing but the people with the necessary funds thought there was no future in automobiles. However, my father continued to build his third car. This car was powered by a two-cylinder, opposed engine, which he obtained from the Buick Motor Co. This was not the automobile co., but they were builders of marine motors. The power from this motor was transmitted to a planetary transmission by chain drive. From sprockets on each end of the gear, roller bearing chains drove the rear wheels to which larger sprockets were attached. These chains and sprockets were all fashioned by my father..."

According to George Hendel's letter, the family drove the third and last car to Minneapolis on their move and continued to use it for several years. "I remember several men coming to look at the car and talking quite a lot. We were finally told a man from Murdoc [sic], South Dakota bought it," George concluded.

A newsclipping from an unnamed paper dated June 14, 1936 is also part of Mike Hendel's collection. It included additional information about the company's brief auto building history.

Better yet, it included a picture of the Hendel touring car loaded down with Hendel family members and suitcases, and another clue to its possible whereabouts: "William H. Hendel, another son ... said the touring car still was in service in the Montana hills in 1910," the article states.

"I think there's a chance the number three vehicle, that took the family to Minneapolis, is still around," Mike Hendel says.

Hendel's identity hangs on by a thread

The tattered remains of an old Hendel ad, and a wooden tool box marked "Wm H Hendel" (inset) helped to identify the car. Dosdall was able to find a copy of the ad in the Dec. 1, 1903, *Cycle and Automobile Trade Journal*. It reads:

"William Hendel & Son of Red Wing, Minn., have placed on the market a strongly constructed gasoline runabout of attractive appearance. This car has a wheelbase of 78 inches and a tread of 56 inches. It weighs 1700 pounds. Power is furnished by a Beilfuss single-cylinder 51/2x6 inches gasoline motor, giving 8 H.P. A Murray transmission gear is used, and power is transmitted from the change speed gear to a Brown-Lipe differential by means of a Baldwin chain. The wood wheels have six spokes each and run on Timken roller bearings. A departure from usual practice is made in the matter of tires. 2 ½-inch Firestone side wire solid tires being used. Steering is accomplished by means of a Brecht steering device.

"The engine is fed by a Kingston carburetor and the exhaust is silenced by a Baldwin muffler. Perfect control of the engine is given by throttling the mixture. Disconnecting the clutch and the brake requires but one movement of the foot and brake lever. The engine is placed under the body and the hood contains the water and fuel tanks and two sets of dry batteries. The machinery is very easily gotten at, and may be quickly removed. The motor is easy to start and is said to never miss fire. The starting cranks is easily reached from the seat. The gasoline tank holds 10 gallons and the water system holds 15 gallons. The car is finished in light maroon, with white trimmings and maroon upholstery. The seat has spring back, slides and cushion stuffed with white hair."

"I'd really like to find it."

Back in Red Wing, Dosdall, who demands proof to be convinced, has looked at the evidence and is impressed. "Look at the front axle," he says, comparing historic photos of his Hendel runabout with the touring car. "The open mouth axle split to fit over the steering line. You can definitely tell it was done by a blacksmith.

"And the hard rubber tires. Most everyone was using pneumatic tires by this time, but he probably thought that air in the tires was nothing but trouble, so he used hard rubber tires like he had always used on his horse drawn wagons.

"And the springs are very fancy. And it has right-hand drive. The one I have has right-hand drive."

Dosdall's conclusion about the touring car photo: "We can't say that it's definitely a Hendel, but it does have the characteristics."

There may, indeed, have been three cars made by William Hendel: The first was likely an experiment that pre-dated the Hendel car company venture. The second was the runabout ordered by the Minneapolis physician and now owned by Dosdall. The third is the missing touring car.

What also seems likely is that another Hendel car was never made after the touring car. Several sources agree on that. According to the 1936 news clipping: "They never built another car. As [son] William explained, 'It was impossible to get capital. Minnesota folk thought the automobile was just a fad.'"

As the debate over the fate of the touring car continues, back in Red Wing, Barry Dosdall has a more immediate dilemma on his hands: does he leave the parts alone and build a replica of the runabout, or does he build a car around the parts that exist? His inclination is to build around the parts. "I have started with less," he says of past restoration projects. He estimates he has 5,000 hours of work ahead of him.

After mulling over how to proceed, Dosdall opted to follow the suggestion of a fellow restorer and draw up a blueprint first so the project could be done as accurately as possible.

When he went to his workshop and pulled down his drafting tools — he had purchased the set at a sale some time ago — he looked at the lid in amazement. On top was written the name "William Hendel." The name had meant nothing to him the day he bought the tools. It means everything to him now.

"I had bought two sets at a sale and one had a name on it and the other one didn't," he recalls. For no particular reason, he sold the set without a name. "I told myself, well, I can paint over the name (on the box), but I didn't, I just stuck it on a shelf."

A coincidence? Yes, and one more curious incident on the Hendel's long and fascinating journey back to Red Wing.

RARE 1923 STUTZ TOURING UNCOVERED

This long-lost 1923 Stutz still has its original paint, upholstery, top and carpeting. All of the mechanical parts, including the engine, gearbox, brakes and electricals, will be rebuilt or recommissioned.

A 1923 Stutz seven-passenger touring, the only known surviving example, was recently acquired by SignificantCars. Com, an established Indianapolis-based collector car brokerage and restoration company. The touring was found in excep-tional, original condition, according to the company.

The Stutz Motor Co. was a mainstay of the Indianapolis automotive world when the Indiana city rivaled Detroit for top status in auto manufacturing operations. More than

"This is the only known 1923 KLHD touring car known to survive."

130 different makes of cars were produced in Indianapolis in the early days of the industry. Stutz cars were produced from 1911 to 1934, and in the marque's heyday, Stutz was one of Indy's "Big 3," along with Marmon and Duesenberg.

Harry C. Stutz was an early automotive entrepreneur, engineer and innovator who grew up repairing agricultural machinery on his family's farm. Automobiles and engines fascinated him, and Stutz built his first car in 1897, then a second automobile using a gasoline engine of his own design and manufacture. In 1905, he designed a car for the American Motor Car Co., and later designed the first transaxle for use at The Marion Automobile Co. In 1911, he designed and built a new car for the inaugural Indianapolis 500, which finished fifth and earned the slogan "the car that made good in a day." He founded an enterprise that he later renamed Stutz Motor Co. He was also instrumental in creating the Stutz Fire Engine Co., as well as the H.C.S. Motor Car Co. in 1919. In 1929, he formed the Stutz-Bellanca Airplane Co.

This 1923 touring is special for several reasons. "1923 was a transitional year for Stutz drivetrains, with the appearance of the new Speedway Six, so very few of the KLDH fours were built in 1923," according to Stutz historian Bill Greer. "This is the only known 1923 KLHD touring car known to survive." The KLHD four is a very stout T-head engine with four valves per cylinder and dual ignition. The engine replaced the original Stutz engine that carried the company through the 1910s. Local upstart rival Duesenberg came out with a straight-eight passenger car engine at this time, so the rugged KLHD four's days were numbered early as cars with six or more cylinders were becoming the fashion.

This car retains its original paint, upholstery, top and carpeting. The wood-framed body is in excellent shape, without wood rot; even the doors shut with authority and do not sag. There is no serious corrosion or rust on any part of the car, and it remains complete. All of the original hardware and gauges are present and well preserved. Most of the original paint still has a good amount of gloss, with the exception of the splash aprons and parts of the fenders. Once a part of the legendary A.K Miller Collection, this car spent the bulk of its life in a barn in Vermont.

The legendary A.K. Miller

A.K. Miller was an eccentric recluse who operated Miller's Flying Service in 1930, in Montclair, N.J. Miller provided mail and other delivery services by means of a gyrocopter, as well as listing "Expert Automobile Repairing" and "Aeroplanes Rebuilt & Overhauled" on his business card. In his later years, he was known for his eccentricities, and his collection of valuable antique cars. After retiring from the Air Force in 1946, Miller and his wife moved to a large farm in East Orange, Vt. It is here that Miller's eccentricities began to emerge. He exchanged most of his cash for gold and silver bars and coins. He took his gyrocopter apart and stored the pieces inside an old one-room schoolhouse that stood on his property. He also constructed a large number of sheds and ramshackle barns out of scrap lumber and nails that he scavenged from various places. Inside the shacks, Miller concealed his trove of prized Stutz motorcars. While locals knew he had a Stutz or two, and Miller was known to other Stutz collectors, nobody knew the true extent of the collection.

What this miserly lifestyle and ill-kept property hid eventually brought $2.18 million at auction. The 87-year-old A.K. Miller himself died in 1993 after falling from a ladder, and Imogene died of a heart attack in 1996. As no heirs were found, the IRS moved in to assess the value of the estate (taking a particular interest in collecting the years of back taxes the Millers had owed). All told, approximately 30 original Stutz motorcars, a Stanley Steamer, a 1926 Rolls-Royce Silver Ghost, several Franklins and assorted Volkswagens were discovered throughout the property. The main barn and the various sheds and shacks Miller had constructed over the years hid a fortune in antique vehicles and a huge number of spare parts Miller had purchased from the Stutz company when it went out of business.

A wood pile hid $1 million in gold bullion while $900,000 in stock certificates and $75,000 in silver bullion and coins were also uncovered in various safes and crawl spaces. A huge, three-day auction was held by Christie's Auction House to liquidate the Miller estate, including the cache of antique and other automobiles, and a cache of other collected items. Today, the A.K. Miller collection is recognized as one of the largest and most well-known collections of Stutz motorcars.

Since the 1923 Stutz touring's purchase from the A.K. Miller estate, it has changed little. Its buyer had just started work on the car, having the wheels repainted, before passing on. His heirs contacted Significant Cars, which jumped at the chance to acquire the car.

Landing a significant car

Significant Cars owner Shawn Miller has a particular interest in Indianapolis-built cars and has several in his collection. Miller is also a champion of original cars.

"Indianapolis produced some very exciting cars during the brass and Classic

"Our approach to this project will be more towards preservation than restoration — it's rare to get that opportunity with a car this old."

era, and having grown up here, it's only natural to want to investigate that and try to preserve that history. I enjoy preserving things, or fixing them up; it's a hobby of mine. I like to find things that have been neglected and breath new life into them," says Miller, who has restored several Victorian buildings in downtown Indianapolis, including an 1880s Veneer Mill that serves as his garage, and more than his fair share of old cars.

"It's refreshing to find a car like this that has so much of its original features intact. Normally, we have to completely disassemble cars of this vintage and start over. "Our approach to this project will be more towards preservation than restoration — it's rare to get that opportunity with a car this old."

All of the mechanical components, such as engine, gearbox, brakes, wiring, etc., will be rebuilt or recommissioned, but great care will be taken to preserve the original finish of all of these items. While the upholstery and top are quite stiff and brittle, Miller says, "We have started the soaking process where we apply various emoluments or salves to the leather and other soft material — I think I can save it, although the top may be another story, since it has been in the folded position so long." Penetrating oil has been liberally applied to all nuts and fasteners that will be removed, so that the originals can be saved and reused if possible.

"We are very excited to get this lovely original car back to its home," Miller said. "This car represents an important part of Indianapolis automotive history that can now be preserved and enjoyed by future generations. I would be remiss if I didn't thank A.K. Miller and the previous owner for keeping the car in such good condition, and of course for passing it on to me."

By Angelo Van Bogart
Photos by Christopher Sauer of KaiserCompany.com

SOMEWHERE EAST OF ANCHORAGE

Long-hidden Jordan Speedway Ace in Cleveland restored to show condition

Only 14 1930 Jordan Model Z series cars were built, and this is the only remaining car. Jim Stecker pulled this Speedway Ace out of its hiding spot 10 years ago, and recently oversaw its lengthy restoration completed for the 2008 Pebble Beach Concours d'Elegance. The car has been out of public view for more than 60 years.

For many years, rumors of a "Cleveland mystery car" circulated around the city, its exact location hidden and precise identity unknown. By the 1970s, at least two people knew that mystery car was a 1930 Jordan Model Z Speedway Ace roadster, one of 14 Model Z's built, and it was in the Cleveland suburb of Collinwood. Among

Owner Jim Stecker finally sits behind the wheel of the car he's
hoped to own and restore since the mid 1970s.

those people who knew about the rare Jordan, a car whose name was made famous by the company's "Somewhere West of Laramie" ads, was well-known car collector and casino owner Bill Harrah. The other was Cleveland car collector Jim Stecker.

How Harrah learned of the "Cleveland mystery car" is probably a secret that died with him in 1978. Surprisingly, Harrah didn't hide the fact that the Speedway Ace still existed, if he was asked about it. However, for those who asked, Harrah did his share to maintain the mystery.

"Harrah said he found it, and it was in Alaska," Stecker said. But all the while, Harrah was paying someone in Cleveland to watch the Speedway Ace after his offer to buy the car was turned down.

Around 1975, Stecker became aware of the Cleveland, Ohio-built Jordan Model Z Series of cars through an article by Ken Gross. In reading the article, Stecker learned that so much excitement surrounded the Model Z, crowds at the New York Auto Show had to wait several hours to get close enough to see them. Despite the public's excitement, only 14 Model Z Series cars were said to be built: 12 Model Z Sports-

The straight-eight was sourced through Continental, and was not unique to Jordan auto-mobiles. The Model Z series of Jordans were inspired by aviation, and the 114-hp engine promised to fly the cars up to better than 100 mph. The engine swallows fuel through a Schebler dual-throat carburetor and is backed by a four-speed Warner Gear transmission.

man sedans and 2 Model Z Speedway Ace roadsters. So few people knew about the Jordan Speedway Ace roadster hidden in Cleveland, even the article stated that none of the cars existed any longer.

Impassioned by reading the article, Stecker went down to a friend's shop and started talking about the Jordans he had just read about. The friend, Weert Ley, said he remembered a Jordan in the Cleveland suburb of Collinwood. Stecker, a self-de-scribed treasure hunter, was immediately on the hunt.

"One day, I was driving around Collin-wood in a 1975 Oldsmobile Toronado with my son Scott," Stecker said. "I came down East 140th Street to an old house with a row of garages, so I pulled in.

"An old man pulled in behind me with a truck," Stecker said. "His name was Laddy Kanker."

It didn't take long for Stecker to sense that Laddy Kanker wasn't interested in making new friends. Immediately, Stecker could tell that Kanker had an untrusting na-ture and preferred to keep to himself, but Stecker felt he was in the right place and wasn't ready to give up.

Set against a solid mahogany instrument panel are all of the aviation-inspired gauges to properly monitor the Jordan Speedway Ace's revolutions, conditions and functions. Included in this attractive cluster, starting with the large gauge at the 10 o'clock position, are an altimeter, temperature gauge, compass, oil pressure gauge, clock, fuel gauge, tachometer and speedometer. The handles in the center of the cluster control spark, choke and throttle, while the controls for the Transitone radio are to the right of the cluster.

"I kept asking him if he had an old car, and I noticed he kept looking at my Toronado. He finally said, 'Yes,' and opened the garage where there was a 1947 Cadillac. But there, out of the corner of my eye, was the Jordan. I saw it and my knees buckled."

Stecker could see that Kanker was nearly as smitten with the Toronado as Stecker was with the Jordan Speedway Ace buried in the corner of the garage. Stecker offered to trade his new Oldsmobile for the Jordan, the only remaining Model Z Series car. No deal.

Stirred by the Speedway Ace's racy looks and its rarity, Stecker did not let the car out of his sight. He spent the next 25 years waiting for the car to become available before landing it in his garage. The car was worth every second of that quarter-century wait,

"I saw it and my knees buckled."

Both Jordan Model Z Speedway Ace models built were true roadsters, each without a provision for a top. To the untrained eye, it appears they were two-seaters, but this is not the case. In this view of the cozy cockpit, a hinge can be seen on the rear deck aft the seat. This hinge allowed a panel to raise, and with the panel raised and passenger seat slid to a forward position, passengers could enter the rumble seat through the passenger's side door.

not just because of its rarity, but because of its ties to Cleveland history.

In 1930, Jordan Motor Car Co. of Cleveland, Ohio, displayed two Model Z Speedway Ace models at auto shows. Car No. 13 went to the New York Auto Show, and Kanker's car, No. 14, went to the Detroit Auto Show in January 1930. At the Detroit show, a man by the name of Harrington bought car No. 14 off the floor for a Depression-scoffing $5,500, a price equivalent to that of some custom-bodied Packards and greater than that of a Cadillac V-16 roadster. Some-

time later, Harrington sold the car to a man named Holloway, who lived on Cleveland's mansion-lined Euclid Avenue. From there, it went to Kanker, who was only 17 or 18 years old at the time of purchase, in 1936.

What Kanker purchased was the last hurrah of a one-time hometown hero. His Jordan Speedway Ace rode on a 145-inch wheelbase exclusive to the Model Z, a fitting alphabetical model designation since this was to be Jordan's last new model. On this imposing chassis stretched a racy, swept-back aluminum roadster body built

by Facto Auto Body Co., also of Cleveland, in a factory once operated by the Chandler Motor Car Co.

The car's long, lithe looks belied its grand size and enormous wheelbase, but an off-the-shelf Continental 12K straight-eight engine of 114 hp ensured the Speedway Ace's speed could match its looks and take its pilot to Laramie or beyond. And probably earn the driver a speeding ticket while doing so.

Equally sleek-looking and trim Woodlite headlamps flanked a shutter-clad radiator that bore no filler cap on top. At the time of the Model Z series' arrival, aircraft were heavily influencing automobile design. In the interest of keeping the Model Z series' styling as clean and aerodynamic as possible, the radiator cap was concealed beneath the hood, which stretched all the way to the windshield. Like the thermostatically controlled radiator shutters, the horizontal hood louvers opened to allow the straight-eight to exhale.

ABOVE: Everything is as sleek inside the Jordan Speedway Ace as it is on the outside. Note the chrome-plated steering column, aviation-inspired instrument cluster and art deco steering wheel. The gauges were expertly restored by John Wolf.

The headlamps, tail lamps and rhyming front fender lamps are all by Woodlite, and each carries the Jordan logo, as does the spotlight. The tail lamp is particularly unique, as it's the only Woodlite tail lamp Stecker has seen, and its design continues the Jordan arrowhead logo.

Fourteen Model Zs were built, and all but this Speedway Ace roadster, pictured in a factory photograph, have two spotlights. Since Stecker's car never had a second spotlight, the car portrayed in this photograph belongs to him. Stecker's car is No. 14 of as many built, so he jokes that the company only had one Jordan-emblazoned spotlight left when his car was built. To bring Stecker's Speedway Ace back to this condition, the expert help of Qual Krom in Erie, Pa., was employed to chrome the new bumpers built for the car, and Art Worledge, president of the Jordan Register, helped make many new castings of emblems, including the Jordan arrowhead on the hubcaps and step plates.

Light fenders over black wall-dressed wire wheels didn't hinder a clear view to the sleek hood louvers. Each fender was a work of art in its own right; a thin, Armani suit-like crease crested all four fenders from tip to tail. Capping off each front fender was a miniature Woodlite lamp that rhymed with the headlamps. On the driver's side rear fender, a Woodlite tail lamp was used, the only such use of a Woodlite tail lamp Stecker has seen. This tail lamp bears

the word "stop" at the top, a clear lens in the center and an upsidedown triangle reminiscent of the Jordan arrowhead-in-a-shield logo at the bottom.

In another nod to the world of aviation, a running board with the profile of an airplane wing was suspended between the unjoined front and rear fenders. Each running board was painted to match the body, striped with thin bright work strips and decked with a lamp on the side (green on the driver's side,

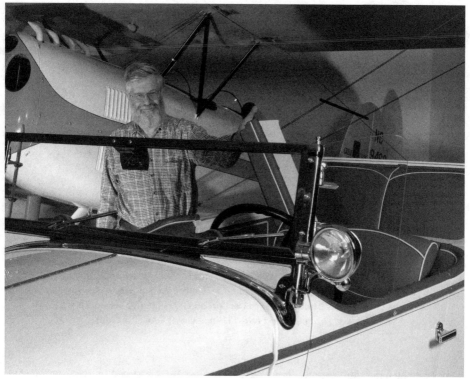

Restorer Jim Capaldi lifts the panel granting access from the front seat to the rumble seat of the 1930 Jordan Model Z Speedway Ace roadster he recently restored.

red on the passenger's side).

Despite his untrusting nature, Kanker and Stecker grew to know each other, and Stecker learned that Kanker had once owned a Model Z Sportsman sedan, which was probably given to a World War II scrap drive for its aluminum body and steel chassis. However, it wasn't until Stecker read Kanker's obituary in 1998 that he learned Kanker had a sister, Janet Lord, in New York City.

Lord was probably more famous than even her brother's rare Jordan had been in 1930. She was an actress and singer who sang for four presidents and appeared in the 1933 Broadway play "Girls in Uniform" and at least one episode of the western "Yancy Derringer" in 1958. When Kanker died, Stecker wrote to Lord and stated he knew Kanker and his Jordan and was interested in purchasing the car. Soon after, Lord placed a call to Stecker and they agreed to meet in Cleveland not more than a quarter mile from where the car was built.

"When Janet walked in anywhere, there was a spotlight on her," Stecker said. "When

Though long and lithe-looking, the Speedway Ace roadster is an imposing car riding on a wheelbase of 145 inches. Like many mechanical parts used on the Speedway Series, the chassis was borrowed from the Jordan Great Line 90 series. To create the chassis, Jordan mated two 132-inch Great Line 90 frames.

I met her at her family home, there were pictures on the mantel. One was Clark Gable with a beautiful brunette, one was Bob Hope with a beautiful brunette, and one was Tyrone Power with the same brunette — that brunette was Janet.

"My dear Connie, the love of my life and my best friend, told me to bring Godiva chocolate to Janet," Stecker said. Within 10 minutes, "We became fast friends, and that's how I bought the car. "When Laddy died, I asked Janet why he kept the car so long," Stecker said. "She said, 'When he got married, he went on his honeymoon with the car. And every time he walked by it, he kicked it.'"

For most of the 60 years Kanker owned the Jordan, it had been hidden in the same garage. Once the title was in Stecker's hands and the car was exposed to the sun again, he could finally properly assess the car's condition, and the prognosis was good. Despite Kanker's foot assaults, the body remained in good condition and the car was driveable. What's more, Speedway Aces only came in ivory (a soft yellow color), and this car retained much of its original paint.

"It only has 35,000 miles, but somewhere along the line, the fenders were thrown away and it was modernized with 1937 LaSalle fenders," Stecker said. For restorer Jim Capaldi of Capaldi Enterprises, recreating the unique fenders originally on the car was one of the most daunting tasks in bringing the

"This was probably the first car that came standard with a radio in it."

Jordan back to the road.

The financially strapped Jordan Motor Car Co. used as many parts from its Great Line 90 series as possible when building the Speedway Aces. However, due to the Speedway Ace's extended wheelbase and custom coachwork, these parts were largely limited to mechanical features. Unfortunately, the parts that needed replacement on Stecker's low-mileage car, such as the fenders, were limited to Model Z-only parts. And since Stecker's Speedway Ace is the only remaining Model Z, acquiring parts from parts cars was out of the question.

"We knew we couldn't find anything, so we didn't look, we reproduced it," Stecker said. "Where are you going to look?"

With no fenders available, Capaldi began the major undertaking of rebuilding the unique and long-gone Speedway Ace fenders out of steel.

He started by making fiberglass fenders to a shape and contour he determined from using photographs as a guide. Through a trial-and-error process, he came up with accurate-looking fiberglass fenders, then took them to George Masavage of Frame Oddities. Masavage created wooden bucks to fit the fiberglass fenders, then slowly pounded and wheeled small sections of metal to fit the bucks. Once the metal panels were

formed, they were welded together to complete each fender. Masavage gave the completed metal fenders to Capaldi, who fitted them to the car.

"If it wasn't for Jim Capaldi, this car would never have been finished. He did a beautiful job."

Crafting new bumpers for the Jordan was less challenging than making new fenders, but Capaldi ran in to a bit of static when it came to the car's Transitone radio, which posed its own restoration speed bumps.

"This was probably the first car that came standard with a radio in it," Stecker said. As a first, or as an early installation of a radio in a car at the least, parts could not be found on dusty, old shelves — they had to be built.

Since Capaldi and Stecker's goal was to bring the last remaining Jordan Model Z Speedway Ace to concours condition, the running engine and transmission were completely rebuilt to original specifications and the chassis was painstakingly detailed.

"I have a brand-new Cadillac and the hood isn't as good as the underneath of this car," Stecker said. Now, his Speedway Ace's show-worthy condition is causing a new problem. Not until after it was restored did Stecker drive the Speedway Ace, and following its maiden voyage, he found himself

"I drove it out of the garage and took it 15 feet, and they yelled at me when I took it back because I got the gas pedal dirty."

in trouble with his restorer.

"I drove it out of the garage and took it 15 feet, and they yelled at me when I took it back because I got the gas pedal dirty. It's polished aluminum and it's beautiful, so they made a protective sleeve for it."

In restoring the car, Capaldi and Stecker did everything in their power to bring the car back to its original configuration, with only one small concession to its current owner's preference. Stecker did not want a black interior in the car once again, so he chose to have it reupholstered by Portage Trim of Ravenna, Ohio, in red leather to an identical pattern. The interior color change required the black highlights on the car's exterior belt line to be changed from black to red in order to match the interior. Overall, the slight changes make for a more visually striking package.

Janet Lord had always hoped to see the car after it was restored and would call Stecker every few months to see if the car was done. Sadly, she passed away last year, just months before the Speedway Ace's restoration was completed. But Stecker knows she'd be happy knowing her introverted brother's magnificent Jordan will once again live an extroverted lifestyle as the star of the show.

LENO LANDS LAST ORIGINAL-OWNER, UNRESTORED DUESENBERG

Jay Leno purchased this 1931 Duesenberg Model J chassis from the son of the original owner. The car shows only 7,000 miles on the odometer, but its 70-year-long storage in a parking garage off New York City's Park Ave. left the car in need of restoration. The car is pictured here upon arrival at Duesenberg historian Randy Ema's Southern California business.

There was once a time when town cars and other formal-bodied cars were unsaleable, often being tossed aside by their original owners whether the cars were used up or not. Those few cars that made it past the first wave of destruction were often employed to haul pigs and other livestock, or undertook other demeaning duties. Sometimes, their bodies were removed altogether and replaced with more sporting coachwork.

Because few people in the position to own a chauffeur-driven car sought "used" examples, finding such a formal car today,

When found, this Duesenberg was completely original. In addition to being subjected on the outside to the poor weather conditions, the interior suffered, because tires were stored in it.

**Other than a missing knob on the steering wheel,
the Duesenberg was remarkably complete, down to its interior.**

on any chassis, is a rarity. But finding a Duesenberg with an untouched town car body, and in the hands of the original family, is downright unheard of, unless you have the right connections.

Jay Leno, best known as host of NBC's "The Tonight Show," is one such person. The comedian is deeply involved in the hobby, and he frequently receives leads on cars. And when a lead includes the word "Duesenberg," Leno's car-hunting divining rod perks up. In this case, the car was a 1931 Duesenberg Model J with a town car body by F.R. Wood and Sons of New York.

"I heard about [the Duesenberg] years ago," he said. "It was one of those rumors you hear about for years and years. I put [this story] in the same category as the 'Corvette that the guy died in that's for sale for $300.' But the interesting thing about rumors is that there's some speck of truth to them."

In this case, the rumors about a Duesenberg parked in a garage off New York's posh Park Ave. were true. To see the car, all Leno had to do was ask the parking garage attendants for a peek.

What he found was a complete, unrestored Duesenberg Model J town car covered in decades of dust.

"For 70 years, one drop of water hit the rear fender."

He tried to buy this car from the original owner's son, but when Leno brought up purchasing the car, the owner changed the subject. After the owner's parking bill grew to thousands of dollars, the owner let the car go to a lien sale, and Leno was able to purchase the Duesenberg from the garage. This Duesenberg joins six others in Leno's collection.

Leno learned from parking ramp employees, including an attendant who had been there 44 years, that the car still belonged to the original owner's son, who had parked the car there in the 1930s.

Despite the low mileage, poor storage conditions had left the town car in need of serious work. Particularly, a leak in the third floor had caused water to drip onto the Duesenberg parked below.

"For 70 years, one drop of water hit the rear fender," Leno said. "It was like Chinese water torture." Additional punishments from Mother Nature affected other parts of the car, too.

Randy Ema, present owner of the Duesenberg company, also had a chance to survey the car while it was in the parking garage. He found the car's paint was buckling off in chunks, the plating was very pit-

Duesenberg town cars are a mix of formality and sport. This especially conservative town-car body rests on an enormously powerful Duesenberg chassis. This is the only F.R. Wood and Sons body fitted to a Duesenberg Model J chassis. One other Classic-era F.R. Wood and Sons body is believed to be fit to a Rolls-Royce chassis.

ted, the trunk rack was broken, and the roof covering had shrunk from the moisture. The driver's compartment covering was also severely damaged, and it came apart when it was retracted for the first time in more than 70 years.

Human contact hadn't helped the Duesenberg's condition, either.

"The right front fender was dented, and that is recent," Ema said. "The interior would have been nice, if there hadn't been tires stored in it." Curious hands also robbed the Duesenberg of its spark control knob on the steering wheel within the last decade. Surprisingly, no one took the radiator cap, hood ornament, or the valuable chronograph.

How the car came to be such a derelict involves a tale of a father and son, a lien, and several unanswered questions.

The Duesenberg was first purchased by a New York department store owner as a chassis from the 1931 New York auto show. Upon purchasing the chassis, the owner had the car delivered to F.R. Wood and Sons for town-car coachwork. Though little known in Duesenberg circles, Wood built a reputation for attractive bodies on other chassis since 1880.

"They were pretty fashionable [in their early days], but by [the time they built this body], their work was pretty conservative,"

"It's not by any means plush; it's pretty plain."

Ema said. But that's probably what the original owner wanted.

"It was 1931, and the market was bad," Ema said. "Once [the original owner] got it, the market got worse, and I think he was worried about looking ostentatious."

Ema pointed out that this town car has the only Wood body on a Duesenberg Model J chassis. It also features some uncommon characteristics.

"This car has an unusual folding-out windshield that hinges out to allow air to get in," Ema said. "It's not by any means plush; it's pretty plain."

Though the car was eventually left to deteriorate, it was well maintained while it was in the hands of the original owner.

"I think they were mesmerized by it, and I think they babied it for a long time," Ema said. "I think he had it serviced and checked over all of the time."

The Duesenberg was also in good company. According to Ema, the son of this Duesenberg's original owner also had a Bugatti Type 57 Atalante and a Rolls-Royce New Market Springfield. Ema has noted several updates and changes to the Wood-bodied Duesenberg that were consistent with factory upgrades conducted until the company shut its doors.

"The common thing with age was that the distributors locked up, and it has a re-placement," Ema said. Even the muffler has been replaced by an improved factory part.

When the son inherited the car, care for it continued — at least initially.

"When the father passed away, the son trailered it up to Jim Hoe's in Connecticut and had new tires put on and the [engine] serviced," Ema said.

From Hoe's famous garage, known for maintaining Rolls-Royces and Duesenbergs after the factory closed, the son drove the car back to New York City. Along the way, he stopped at a Classic Car Club of America meet. For some reason, the car never put its tires back on to the street once it was back in New York City.

Even aside from its special story, the town car is a remarkable vehicle. It was the last unrestored Duesenberg to remain in the hands of its original owner's family.

"There are other Duesenbergs that are in original condition that are not original-owner cars, and there is another original-owner car, but it's not in original condition," Ema said. "This is the last original-owner, original-condition car."

While the Duesenberg sat parked through several presidential administrations, its parking bill continued to grow along with the U.S.'s budget deficit. When Leno learned that the Duesenberg would be available for sale through a lien by the park-

"It's a real piece of history."

ing garage, he missed the sale. Fortunately, the garage didn't have the paperwork in order, so he had a second chance to purchase the car. But he wasn't the only one hot on the Duesenberg's trail.

"I was not the first one to hear about it for sale, but I think everyone assumed [the garage owners] didn't know the car's value," Leno said. The parking garage was low-balled by several parties, and their offers were turned down by the garage owners. When Leno went after the car, he showed up with the documentation to reflect the car's true value and to make a fair offer.

"I went to the garage and said, 'I'm a collector, and I'm not going to sell it. Here's what it's probably worth.'" His offer to purchase this important piece of history was accepted.

"The thing about this car is it's too far gone to keep original," he said. "It is the last original-owner car, but unlike the Model X I bought, this sat in a damp New York garage."

A comprehensive restoration will take some time. "We've soaked the engine and filled it with oil so it will come apart easy," Ema said. "We've made up new water plates and a water pump."

Ema and his crew have also taken steps to repair or replace the rusted fenders, as well.

Although the car is not a sporty speedster or a capricious coupe, Leno is very happy with the Duesenberg.

"Duesenbergs are like pizza — even if it's not very good, it's still pizza," Leno said. "Ultimately, is a town car my favorite body? [If it were sportier], that would make it worth 10 times what I paid for it."

While the town car's styling isn't the most beautiful body type, Leno appreciates its uniqueness.

"When I get in it, it's different. [A town car offers] a driving experience you can't replicate in any car. When you're in it, you can have the top open or closed."

Leno also enjoys explaining the antiquated body style to people unfamiliar with prewar cars.

"It's a real piece of history," Leno said.

And it will be a piece of history that will again be treasured by a caring owner, just as it was in 1931.

Story update

By 2009, the restoration of Jay Leno's F.R. Wood and Sons-bodied Duesenberg Model J town car was completed by Randy Ema and his staff at Randy Ema, Inc.

LENO AND SHAPPY DISCOVER TWO DUSTY DUESENBERGS

In late 2004, this Duesenberg was pulled out a Boston-area carriage house where it had rested since 1950. (Dick Shappy collection)

Every automobile enthusiast probably dreams of finding a rare or desirable car forgotten in a remote barn, scooping it up for a paltry sum, dusting off 50 years of neglect, and having a great story to tell at club meets and car shows.

For collectors around the world, the Duesenberg is the ultimate American car, and to locate one of these ultra-rare, powerful, and justifiably desirable cars hidden in a building is the ultimate find.

In late 2004, two collectors made such discoveries, and on opposite coasts of the U.S. Collector Dick Shappy, who is known for his excellent prewar Cadillac restorations, and car collector and TV personality Jay Leno each found Duesenbergs that had been hiding for more than 50 years near

their homes. Both concluded a deal with their owners, with plans to re-introduce their cars to the highways and to the hobby.

Because of their beauty, raw power, and sophisticated design, Duesenbergs are considered among the most exotic automobiles in the world. The cars are so rare that historians have counted the remaining cars and can instantly recognize a specific Duesenberg from a photo, old or new, and recite its serial number and history. To unearth examples would be the hobby's equivalent of finding Noah's ark to the archeological world. Yet, Shappy and Leno did just that. Obviously, it's not something that happens everyday, let alone twice in one year, but 2004 was blessed with the recovery of two Duesenbergs. Here are their stories.

The carriage house-cloaked J

Shappy appreciates many types of cars, but he is best known for his quality restorations of Classic Cadillacs. Shappy has always dreamed of owning a Duesenberg, but it is not a car he thought he would ever see parked in his garage because of their rarity and value. Luckily, fate had a different plan for his future, and in 2004, a conversation started him on the path to Duesenberg ownership.

"I had gotten an e-mail that said a Duesenberg was coming up for sale," Shappy said. "I've wanted a Duesenberg all my life, and my wife knew. When I told her there was a Duesenberg for sale, she told me to go for it. I'm very happy I did." A request for more information from the message's sender produced quick results.

The Duesenberg as it appeared when the Cades bought the car from Duesenberg dealer John Troka in 1941 for $450.

"I said I'd like to learn more about it, and the next thing you know, Dan LaCroix (the broker involved in the Duesenberg's sale) called me and said, 'I got a call from a gentleman who said you might be interested in buying the car,'" Shappy said. Doubting the car was indeed a Duesenberg, Shappy requested that the broker send him some photos over the weekend.

In the meantime, Shappy called noted Duesenberg authority Randy Ema about the car. Shappy said Ema told him, "You'd better not let that thing sit there long. When everybody finds out it's for sale, it won't be there long."

Throughout the weekend, Shappy checked his computer to see if the photos had been sent, but each time he checked, he logged off disappointed. A check of his e-mail the following Monday morning still didn't yield photos from the broker. But at 10 a.m., Shappy again looked through his e-mail and found several photos from LaCroix. The images in the messages verified what Shappy hoped: the car was a Duesenberg.

The car carried a Derham convertible sedan body stripped of its paint and a few other items, but it was certainly within the realm of restoration and definitely worth further inquiries. Shappy quickly picked up the phone and contacted the broker to make arrangements to see the car.

The broker suggested that he, Shappy, and the owner meet later in the week, but Shappy insisted that they meet that Monday. After the broker agreed, Shappy quickly dressed and prepared for the short jaunt to Boston from his Rhode Island home.

Within two hours, Shappy was at the three-story brick carriage house of Mrs. Margaret Cade. The brick building was a true time capsule unto itself. Upon entering the building, Shappy noticed names of horses above the stalls from the time when the building was home to horses instead of a valuable car. The walls of the carriage house were lined with racing posters from the 1940s, and Shappy would soon learn that they had a special meaning in this Duesenberg's life. When he finally laid eyes on the Duesenberg, he noticed that the parts missing in the photographs were hanging on the car, which was recently placed on a set of rollers to aid his inspection.

The apple green straight-eight engine was resting next to the car in pieces. But, like the rest of the car, it was complete. Cade's husband, Phil, had started rebuilding the engine in the 1950s, but some time in the early '60s, he lost interest in the project.

The broker and the friend that gave him the lead told Shappy that the car was intact and had been sitting, but Shappy had no idea what it would look like. To say Shappy was pleased with the car would be a gross understatement.

"When I saw the car, I fell in love." he said. "I like them crusty, (and) I like it when they need my attention. That's my purpose: to bring cars back from the dead. I really appreciate them when they're original or apart, because that's what I do."

This Duesenberg was hardly dead, it was a little beaten down, and definitely crusty and in need of attention.

The paint on the Derham convertible sedan body had been stripped in the 1940s, exposing its aluminum construction, though the fenders retained their aged maroon color. It was one more piece of a puzzle that would soon be complete.

From Ema, Shappy learned the car had been bought new by a Mr. Offield, a cousin to the multiple Duesenberg-owning Wrigley family. Cade continued the tale of the Duesenberg through several old photos of the car and family. It seems that the Cades bought the car from John Troka for $450 in 1941, and the car became Cade's daily driver. After the Cades moved to Boston, Margaret Cade drove the car to visit her daughter at school in Iowa, and on other occasions she and some of her friends would hop in the Duesenberg for a weekend out on the town. At least one of Cade's trips with the Duesenberg involved a small disaster.

"The car caught fire on the rear seat after filling it up," Shappy said of Cade's trip to Iowa. "It did involve the fire department,

Dick Shappy stopped for a photo with Mrs. Margaret Cade, who, along with her deceased husband, owned the Duesenberg for more than 60 years. The car sat in her carriage house undriven since at least 1950.

and some of the leather was wrecked. You can still see where there was a fire."

Luckily, the car was not structurally harmed, and even today, Shappy reports that there's, "not a hint of rust, and the wood is as solid as the day they made it."

Mr. Cade, an engineer, eventually took over the Duesenberg and decided to stretch the car's legs at Watkins Glen International raceway in Watkins Glen, New York, after the family moved to Boston. Cade stripped the black paint off the Derham convertible sedan's aluminum body, removed the fenders and top, and painted the number 10 on

the car's side. In Shappy's opinion, "the car didn't look like a race car at all." However, in 1949, the car placed 28th in the annual race at Watkins Glen.

"He raced the thing for a couple of races," Shappy said. "There was no wear and tear on the car; time just caught up with it (and it couldn't compete)."

Apparently disappointed with the J's inability to keep up with the smaller, quicker competition, Cade bought a Maserati shortly thereafter and raced that. But he wasn't done with the Duesenberg. He re-installed the convertible top and fenders, and put

Shappy's Duesenberg as it appears today.

Packard bumpers on the front and rear of the Duesenberg to push his Maserati around the pits. He also added a trailer hitch so that the Duesenberg could be used to pull his new sports car to the race track. The Duesenberg's jockeying duties didn't last long, and the car was parked within a year.

More than 50 years later, and after a brief examination of the car, Shappy and Cade had made a deal and the car was ready to see the light of day for the first time in more than 50 years.

Shappy worked quickly to get the Duesenberg ready to drive next summer. He replaced the bumpers with original Duesenberg units purchased from Ema and began rebuilding the engine with help from Brian Joseph and Sean Brayton, Shappy's mechanics. The car went to a restoration shop for paint. Shappy uncovered the original colors, which he refers to as a "horrendous" olive drab, and he's not yet sure if he will return the car to that shade. The ancient tires have also been replaced and mounted on rechromed wheels. The rest of the car will remain in original condition, including the bulk of the chrome.

"Maybe 10 people have offered to buy it from me, but it's not for sale. I'm putting the car back together and driving it," Shappy said.

Story update

Dick Shappy has remained true to his word: The Duesenberg has been sympathetically restored with new two-tone green paint in the origin colors and new upholstery, but the chrome, paint on the frame and other components remain unrestored. He retains the car today.

Leno's mysterious Model X

In an unlikely coincidence, a similar formula of discovery transpired, this time, on the opposite coast of the U.S.

Like Shappy, Jay Leno uncovered a forgotten Duesenberg, and not far from his home.

Leno had heard there was an old car tucked in a southern California garage, and he decided to approach the owner one day while he was out touring in his Stanley steamer. The owner greeted Leno, but he would not show him what he was hiding in the garage. Even after several conversations with the gentleman at his home over the course of 20 years, Leno did not know exactly what was in the garage.

Although content that he had at least made a friend over the years, Leno caught a break in finally uncovering the mystery in the garage. The older gentleman had moved to a retirement home and decided that the time had come to allow Leno to see his secret. With the help of the owner's daughter, Leno finally walked into the garage to see what had been hiding under wraps. The daughter herself hadn't been in the two-car, stuccoed garage since 1950 and only knew that there was an "old car" parked in it. The anticipation had grown, and before he saw the old car, Leno told her he didn't care what it was, he just wanted to buy it.

When the door was finally lifted, he laid eyes on a large sedan surrounded by old newspaper clippings declaring "Japs attack Pearl Harbor," empty oleomargarine jars, porcelain signs, and other artifacts that made the garage look like a tomb that hadn't been opened since the '40s. The dark blue sedan turned out to be an example of America's premier automobile, and one of its rarest. Not only was the car a fabled Duesenberg, but it was a Model X, one of just 13 produced by the Indianapolis company.

"I was thrilled it was in as nice of shape as it was," Leno said. "It's a real 'car-in-a-barn' story.

"I grew up in a small town with stories about cars hidden in barns. There was always a World War II Jeep in Cosmoline, but it never turned out to be true, so the fact this story really was true was exciting."

Of the 13 Model X's, only four remain. Two of those X's are Locke sedan bodies, like Leno's car. The third is a Locke dual-cowl phaeton, and the fourth is the single McFarland-bodied speedster built.

How a Southern California man came to own such a rare automobile and store it for more than 50 years is actually a tale about the car collecting hobby's infancy.

When living in Chicago in the late 1930s, the gentleman began collecting Duesenbergs. He was in the right place since there was a factory distributor of the marque in that city, and it was close to Jim Troka, a car collector and dealer who dealt in Duesen-

Jay Leno uncovered this Locke-bodied Duesenberg Model X sedan in a California garage near his home. The car had been parked since 1947. (Randy Ema collection)

bergs and Rolls-Royces when they were just "used cars" in the 1940s. In the late 1930s and into the '40s, the gentleman secured at least three Model A Duesenbergs and, finally, this Locke-bodied Model X sedan. When the gentleman moved to California, the Model X followed him, but not under its own power. Since the it was not in running condition, the man had the car shipped via rail to California, then dragged the car to his home behind his Model A dual-cowl phaeton.

While in his care, the Model X was not driven. Or painted. Or reupholstered. Nor did it need any of it. The owner simply parked it, still draped in its original paint, rolled up the windows to preserve the original interior, and left the car to age like a fine wine. The garage preserved all of the car's original features, with the help of the California climate.

The owner finally agreed that he had kept the Model X long enough, and made a deal with Leno to sell the car. Luckily, Leno appreciates fine original features, and will not be restoring the Duesenberg. Instead, he and his friend, Ema are cleaning up 50 years worth of dust on the body and in the interior.

"I'll drive the car and use the car," Leno said. "I don't care if it gets an award.

"This is the first I've found that's nice enough that it doesn't have to be restored. This is the only unrestored car in my collection that still has its original paint. They're only new once.

Today, the largely original Model X Locke sedan (right) stands tall among Leno's other restored Classics, including the A.H. Walker Body Co.-built Model J coupe (left).

"The nice thing about this car was it didn't need a complete restoration," Leno said, adding that it did require some mechanical work. "Others I've found in the past have had to be ground-up restored. Or 80 percent of the time, they have to be re-restored, because they weren't intended to be driven and the bolts weren't tightened in order to avoid cracking the paint."

More than 55 years of storage are difficult on any car, and Leno's Duesenberg is no different.

"We started looking, and it (the engine) was nothing but trouble," Ema said. "We had to scrap the rods. We had to bore the engine, make a whole new distributor, and the front axle was cracked. Tons of stuff had to be done that we didn't plan on, but we're bringing it back."

Maintaining a car's mechanics is completely acceptable and expected in shows and clubs that welcome original and unrestored cars. Except for the rear axle, all of this Model X's mechanics.

"It will have a painted up motor, but everything on the outside will be original. We're not touching the hood or radiator shell, and the interior is very nice; (there's) not a pinhole in it. Fortunately, they left the windows up, otherwise the moths would have eaten it up," Ema said.

"The car had a peach can for a gas cap, so we made a new one and plated it," Ema said. "It has 1940 Ford-style bumpers, so we'll make new bumpers for it."

The Model X also had small, incorrect headlights on it when Leno purchased the car, but Ema had a correct set and installed them on the car. Other than these small details, the exterior and interior of the car is as it was built by Locke and Duesenberg for an unknown original owner, who is thought to have lived in Indiana.

In fact, until the car was owned by Troka, little is known about its history, and in general, less is known about Model X's than their Model A predecessors and Model J contemporaries.

"I figure, around 1940, somebody dragged it out, did some homebrew work to get it on the road, but they really screwed things up," Ema said. "It was just crude work. They tried to get the brakes to work, [and the result of their work was that] the front axle filled with brake fluid. By 1947, it ended up in Chicago and Troka offered it for sale."

Ema also believes that this was a show car, "Because it had a polished oil pan and transmission, which, in most Model Xs, they are not (polished)." The block on Leno's Model X was also filled with filler to make the surface smooth.

Ema said no early photos exist of either one of the Locke-bodied sedans, nor does he or any other Duesenberg historians know where this car was displayed when it was shown. Because of its attention to chassis detail, he believes it was used to show custom coachwork elements.

With Leno's Model X in his shop alongside another owner's Model A, the differences between the cars was easy to see. "It's been interesting to compare the Model A in our shop and the Model X. You can see some of their logic where they would see things that wouldn't work," Ema said. Because Model A's and X's were built in-house, the engineers could readily see how components worked in a car, and then modify or redesign them for improvement. With an in-house machine department, this also aided in developing the Duesenberg into the ultimate automobile.

Since the Model X is a transitional car between the Model A and Model J, it's not surprising that most of the mechanical parts on the Model X are modified Model A parts. It is surprising, however, that few if any parts are interchangeable between cars, making the 13 Model X's unique.

According to Ema, the straight-eight engine blocks are nearly the same from Model A to X, and there are some significant changes. And while the pistons and rods are the same, the valve angle was changed on the Model X, allowing the engine to have more of a hemispherical combustion chamber. These changes provided the Model X with a 12 hp increase over the Model A's figures for an even 100 hp in the Model X.

Leno's story, along with that of Shappy, prove that cars are still out there, waiting to be found, and if it's true for one of America's rarest and sought-after automobiles, then there's hope of finding that '67 Mustang, '56 Corvette, or '42 Studebaker on your wish list.

Story update

Like Shappy and his Model J, Jay Leno has elected to keep his Model X sedan as original as possible. The car's mechanical components have been restored to make the car functional, but the remainder of the car has been preserved in original condition.

By Coy Thomas

EARLY V-8 FORDS FOUND IN REMOTE FARMHOUSE

ABOVE: A sight not often seen today is that of the instantly identifiable nose of a 1936 Ford hiding in a long-forgotten farmstead.

RIGHT: The interior of this 1936 Ford Standard coupe is a little dirty from sitting, but it is complete and ready for refurbishing.

This 1936 Ford Standard five-window coupe was found in the basement of the farmhouse and is a very complete car that will need a lot of work, but it is certainly restorable.

In August of 2004, Rick Bennebohm, an avid car collector and enthusiast who worked at Frontier Chevrolet-Pontiac in Oak Harbor, Wash., received a call that some old Fords had been found resting quietly in an overgrown remote farmhouse.

Bennebohm quickly packed his overalls and flashlight to follow the directions to the old tomb holding the secret of vintage Fords. He was hoping his informant had correctly identified the cars as Fords, especially early V-8s. If they were Fords, it would be a royal find.

Upon arriving at the farm, Bennebohm approached the old buildings through the maze of brush and debris. As he circled the collapsed shed, he noticed it was covering a '36 Ford five-window coupe. After moving numerous pieces, he noticed it was a Deluxe coupe complete with 1949 license plates, a radio, its banjo wheel, and its Deluxe garnish mouldings.

The tour guide then told Bennebohm that the coupe in the shed must be a parts car for the other car stored in the basement. Bennebohm quickly followed him to the basement, pried open its door, moved several pounds of items from in and around the rear of the car, and discovered another 1936 Ford coupe, this time a Standard model complete

The guide who led Rick Bennebohm to the pair of 1936 Fords left forgotten on a farmstead identified this Deluxe coupe as a parts car for a second, but it, too, could be restored.

with a homemade sign attached to the rear tailpan that said, "More jobs — save our salmon."

Both coupes were complete with their flatheads and mechanical brakes. However, each needed a frame-up restoration by an ambitious early V-8 restorer.

The possibility of locating two unrestored and untouched 1936 Ford coupes this day in age is a rarity, but Bennebohmk can now say he has had that opportunity!

The Deluxe coupe wears 1949 license plates and this sign, "More jobs: Save Our Salmon."

Story by Dick Downing

DIVINE INTERVENTION

Chance church meeting leads to stellar stash of vintage iron

This 1928 Marmon Model 68 was relatively simple to get running again. The car was also solid, but it needed an interior and was sold to another collector before it was finished.

In 2005, a person in my church asked if I could help him in disposing of his deceased father's old cars. Not knowing what I was getting into, two friends and I went with him from our Indianapolis home to the Detroit area and found four storage units full of partially disassembled cars and tons of parts. Also at his home was a workshop full of parts and tools. His widow had already sold several old Volkswagens and Mercedes-Benz models from the 1960s. We had only a week to empty the storage

I made an offer for the lot and she accepted with the provision that a 1949 MG-TC be assembled to running condition for her grandsons — a challenge we accepted.

units. This time period was too short for an auction or bids, so I made an offer for the lot and she accepted with the provision that a 1949 MG-TC be assembled to running condition for her grandsons — a challenge we accepted.

We then assembled a convoy of three pickups and trailers and started sorting and loading. The MG was totally apart and in 35 different boxes, along with many other car parts. A late-1931 Ford Model A pickup was likewise apart with its pieces scattered. A Marmon sedan from the collection was missing its bumpers and interior upholstery, and a Blackhawk coupe was partially apart and its pieces were scattered. Not knowing

The author had to collect and assemble most of the pieces
to a 1931 Ford pickup and a 1949 MG-TC.

for sure what parts belonged to each car further compounded the project. We did the best we could and loaded the parts for a trip back to my workshop in Indiana. We then went back and found more parts in his workshop basement and a loft. Luckily, we found nearly all the remaining parts for the four cars.

The Marmon was easy to get running. We had to make several replacements for various die-cast zinc parts that had failed, and we also had to repair the entire fuel system and install an electric fuel pump. The Marmon was a low-mileage example

and ran very well, except for a bad rear oil seal leak. I removed the oil pan and found a very clean engine; I don't believe it had ever been worked on before. I removed the rear bearing cap and discovered that this engine had inserts for main bearings, and also a removable seal gland, which had an easily made cork seal. The inside of the engine was perfect with no damage to the cylinder walls. I reassembled and checked compression — it was to the original specifications. This is a flathead straight-eight engine of about 215 cubic inches in displacement. It started up just fine with no oil leaks and ran

The Blackhawk was found still wearing its original green and black paint.
The missing sheet metal was also located, and it's currently undergoing a restoration.

very quiet.

The Marmon's woodwork was good and there was no rust on the body. It had a trunk with a spare clutch plate, gasket set, spark plugs and tune-up kit, grease gun and jack. It also had new tires. I did not want to try to upholster this car, so I sold it to a collector from Iowa who had it upholstered. He now drives it regularly in parades and shows.

The Model A truck was complete, but it had many bad parts and other problems, so I decided to sell it to a Model A parts dealer that I know in Illinois.

The MG was quite a challenge. The deceased owner had purchased it new while he was stationed in England after World War II, but he had run it hard and it was rough. It had been apart for about 15 years, but we found about many NOS parts for it. We did manage to reassemble it and install a new wood kit in the body, and started on the bodywork when we discovered a serious problem with the engine. It had a loose wrist pin that had ruined the block even beyond sleeving, and the instrument panel wiring and instruments were a mess. At that point, we sold the project to an MG collector and the widow was happy with the money she received for it.

We decided to keep the last car from the

collection, a Blackhawk coupe. The Blackhawk was manufactured by the Stutz car company as a lower-cost companion car to the regular Stutz line. The deceased owner had bought it about 60 years ago as his first car, which he drove in high school until the late 1940s. It has been in storage ever since. He started to restore it in 1990 and then it sat. The Blackhawk has about 58,000 miles and the engine runs just fine.

The Blackhawk is an interesting car, as its engine has an overhead camshaft, chain-driven operation directly on the valves, and a second duplex chain drives an accessory shaft with the distributor, generator, water pump and fan, so no belts are required. The car's six-cylinder engine displaces 252 cubic inches and has a seven-main-bearing crankshaft and aluminum pistons and connecting rods. The radiator has thermostatically controlled shutters.

The car has a chassis oiling system, worm-drive differential, a four-speed transmission with a no-back feature and constant mesh, so no double-clutching is required. The car has very large hydraulic brakes with a vacuum booster and an instrument panel control for booster pressure.

The paint is original, and the body has no rust and the framework has no wood rot. The upholstery is original and in poor condition. Currently, we are in the process of reworking the fenders and running boards, which had some rust damage. The work to make it a good driver is near complete. We have had to make many parts that were missing or in poor condition, especially die-cast parts.

Here in Indianapolis, the buildings in which the Marmon and the Blackhawk were assembled still stand, and I have stood at the very spot my Blackhawk was built. The Stutz complex of buildings is owned by a local businessman and car collector, and they are in very good original shape and can be toured any time.

Perhaps when the Blackhawk is back to its original glory, the car will tour to the complex.

AUBURN ALLURE

'Barn-find' 1935 Speedster helps revive collector's love for Classic marque

A chance meeting in a parking lot eventually led Connecticut Auburn connoisseur John Pascucci to purchase this splendid 1935 Auburn Speedster. The car had been stored for five decades by a previous owner. (Photos by Beth Miller, Generations Photography)

When it comes to car collecting, John Pascucci admits he's had a pretty charmed life. In the early years of the Classic car hobby's exponential growth, he was right there with his father, pulling Duesenbergs out of parking garages and Isotta-Fraschinis out of dank places. But he never thought more than 40 years later, following the passing of his father, he'd experience a

"great find" of his own — a 1935 Auburn Speedster walled into a garage at the end of a dirt driveway since the early 1960s.

"If you told me three years ago I would be doing what I am today and finding an Auburn, I'd say that's far fetched," Pascucci said. "It's a nice omen telling me I'm doing what I should be."

About 10 years ago, when Pascucci's

father, Anthony, grew ill, the two men stopped dabbling in the hobby while the younger Pascucci began caring for his dad. After Anthony passed, John kept a low profile, ignoring even the Auburn Speedster Anthony had bought for him as a teenager. But then the love for the hobby instilled in Pascucci by his father decades earlier took hold, and he found himself driving to the Fall Auburn auction.

"I saw a small little mention in a brochure that this Auburn tucked away since the '50s was going to be at Auburn," said Pascucci, a resident of Meriden, Conn. The bronze Speedster never made it to the 2008 auction, but Pascucci was fortunate to see the car on a trailer in a parking lot in that city. He stopped to talk to the people hauling the car and learned that he wasn't the only passerby to stop and check out the Auburn.

"A lot of people wanted to buy it, but [the owners] didn't have the paperwork and so they brought it back where they found it," Pascucci said.

The visit in the Auburn parking lot became a learning experience. Pascucci found out the car's owner, Alonzo B. Smith, had died 15 years ago, and he had bought the Auburn when he was just 16 from the son of a doctor in 1948. The front of the car was wrecked when Smith purchased the car, but he had the metal replaced. The car also featured a professionally installed 1937 Ca-

Though he can't be sure, the car's owner believes the streamlined Auburn may have been raced in the 1940s or '50s.

dillac engine and 1937 Chrysler Royal rear end, though it's unclear if Smith, an accomplished mechanic, bought the car with these drivetrain modifications, had them installed or did the work himself. While Smith kept excellent records of the modifications, he didn't date the time period in which the work was undertaken.

Smith drove the refurbished Auburn until 1951, when he was drafted to serve in the Korean War, and only occasionally after he returned from the conflict. He then tucked the car away in the early 1960s.

"They literally poured a cement slab, parked the car on it and built a garage around it," Pascucci said. "The garage only had one door on the left [and the car was parked on the right] so they had to move it with jacks."

While standing in the Auburn parking lot, Pascucci made an offer to purchase the car from Smith's children and left them with his phone number. He didn't learn until several months later whether or not his offer had been accepted.

"One November day, I got a phone call from a woman in her 70s, and she said, 'You made a fair offer and you can have it,'" Pascucci said. The woman was the late Auburn owner's widow, and Pascucci didn't

The Speedster received a 1937 Cadillac engine at some point in its life.

waste any time. "I got in my truck and drove through a snowstorm to Akron, Ohio," he said.

To say Pascucci knows Speedsters is an understatement. Pascucci and his father have combined to own 12 such Auburns.

"I was six or seven when my dad bought his first Auburn, and we've always had two or three," Pascucci said. When he spotted the bronze Auburn Speedster in the Auburn parking lot, Pascucci knew exactly what he was looking at: a very solid car with professional — and reversible — period modifications.

Pascucci believes that, after the engine was installed in the Auburn, the car may have been raced around Ohio in the late 1940s or 1950s, but he has not yet been able to confirm his suspicions.

"This car might have been raced by Jack Rutherford at Daytona in the 1940s, which might explain the Cadillac engine and the car being wrecked at the time of purchase," Pascucci said. "His son tried to trace back the history on the car after his father passed away, and he was able to eliminate almost all but approximately 15 Auburns that might have been raced at Daytona, one of them possibly being this automobile."

Regardless of its past, the Speedster remains a remarkable find. "To me, this Auburn is a great find, because they are so hot

"I was six or seven when my dad bought his first Auburn, and we've always had two or three."

right now, and this car was in a quiet town in an old neighborhood parked in a garage with a dirt driveway," Pascucci said. "It wasn't a car anybody really knew about, or those who did have passed away."

While Pascucci is hesitant to make changes to the Speedster, he's replacing some of the car's few missing pieces by digging through his own long-stored spare parts for correct components — and he's having a great time doing it.

"I am going through boxes and finding parts, [such as] knobs, a hood ornament and other pieces, to replace the few missing items," Pascucci said. His goal is to bring the garage-find Speedster and the magnificently restored Auburn his father bought him long ago to the Auburn Cord Duesenberg Club Reunion in 2009.

"The car will probably be restored some day," he said, "but I might massage it and bring it like it is. I might get the right engine and leave it with the car, but [the Cadillac engine] runs so good and they did such a beautiful job [installing it]; nothing was cut or modified. I don't know what my plan is, but I am going to gather all of the parts I can to make it correct."

Networking to find parts shouldn't be difficult. As the owner of Johnny P's Classic Cars, a collector-car dealership, Pascucci's connections extend beyond even those formed when he was a child, tagging along with his father from garage find to barn find. From those old friends, he's already been receiving all the encouragement he could ask for.

"What makes it exciting for me, after I lost my parents and my brother, everybody has been trying to get me back in the hobby," he said. "Since getting back in the hobby, it's been like a warm hug."

Even though he hasn't had his new Speedster very long, the connections to family and friends of the past and present have sparked a special bond between Pascucci and the car. It's a bond he'd like to extend to the next generation.

"I am thinking about keeping it," Pascucci said. "My daughter is six and I thought about restoring it with her as a father-daughter project."

Regardless of whether a "for sale" sign ever hangs from the Speedster's art deco rearview mirror, we're sure Pascucci's father would be proud.

A WOODIE GOOD FIND

Collector beats termites to woodie duo hidden in semi trailer

John Katerba remembered this 1939 Plymouth station wagon from his youth, and a chance meeting with its longtime owner resulted in Katerba purchasing the car.

Since he was young, Monroe Township, N.J resident John Katerba knew a local farmer owned a 1939 Plymouth woodie. The car didn't strike him in his youth, as he had two sons and his high school car, a 1969 Chevelle, to take care of. But a chance meeting with the Plymouth owner in 2007 got him thinking about the woodie again.

"I always knew that the farmer had it, but I had no interest in it about 15 years ago," Katerba said. "I ran into Bob, the farmer, while paying my taxes and I asked if he still had the Plymouth and if we could look at it. He said, 'Sure, I haven't been down to look at it for a while. That would be fun.'"

Later, the two men drove out to the mid-

"The seller said, 'Give me $500 for both,' so the farmer bought both cars and pushed the Ford in the trailer."

dle of the farmer's 50-acre field to a lone semi trailer that served as the Plymouth's garage. When the trailer door was opened, Katerba was stunned. Not only was the 1939 Plymouth parked in the trailer, but behind it was an equally dusty 1948 Ford Super Deluxe woodie he had never seen or heard of before.

"It was like opening King Tut's tomb," Katerba said of the two treasures. "They were covered with cobwebs and dust."

Katerba learned the farmer had no interest in purchasing the Ford when he bought the Plymouth for $1,500 in the early 1970s, but when the farmer tried to buy only the Plymouth, he was presented with an offer he couldn't refuse.

"The farmer did not want to buy the Ford, he just wanted to buy the '39 in the ad," said Katerba. "The seller said, 'Give me $500 more for the Ford,' so the farmer bought both cars [for $2,000] and pushed the Ford

in the trailer." Meanwhile, the Plymouth was given a new coat of paint and driven, at least for a few years.

Unlike the Plymouth, the Ford woodie was left to gather dust in the trailer since the farmer had obtained it in 1972. But like the farmer, Katerba was originally interested in only the Plymouth and made an offer to purchase it. Katerba and the farmer came to an agreement, and Katerba brought home a very well preserved, largely original 30,000-mile 1939 Plymouth station wagon that he soon learned was rather rare. Currently, only two or three are listed in the Plymouth Club roster.

"I bought the Plymouth, because it was all complete and there was no hunting for parts," he said.

Immediately, Katerba set out to make the Plymouth roadworthy again.

"We towed that car out of there, and after about five months, I got the whole thing running," he said. "I had it rewired with a new wiring harness with the cloth covering from Rhode Island Wiring. I bought pre-bent stainless-steel brake lines from Classic Inline Tube and replaced the gas tank."

After other small projects over a five-month period, Katerba had the Plymouth on the road again, and was able to retain many of the vehicle's original parts in the process.

"It has the original voltage regulator, starter and radiator," Katerba said. "I

Katerba had no idea the Plymouth's owner was hiding this 1948 Ford station wagon Eventually, he purchased the Ford, too.

cleaned the contacts, did a valve job, got new hoses, brakes, brake springs, wheel cylinders, flushed the rear, flushed the transmission, and now it's a great car to drive. It's not perfect, but I put the kids in there and go to soccer games."

Unforgettable Ford found

After a couple years behind the wheel of the 1939 Plymouth woodie station wagon, Katerba couldn't shake the thought of that Ford that had kept the Plymouth company in the trailer. In the meantime, he had shown

the Plymouth's previous owner all the work he had done on the car, so he wasn't shy about inquiring about a possible sale of the Ford woodie.

"Two years go by and I keep thinking about that Ford, so I went back and asked the owner about it, he said, 'You already got one of my cars — I want to keep the other.'"

What commenced after that might constitute stalking, Katerba joked, but his persistence paid off.

"I guess I wore him down far enough,

"This was luck. That's all it was."

and he figured he was not going to restore the Ford, and he was impressed with how I got the Plymouth done when I took it by him," Katerba said.

On April 5, 2009, Katerba and his family drove back to that lone trailer in the New Jersey field and pulled out its last treasure, a 1948 Ford Super Deluxe woodie station wagon, also in very much original and well-preserved condition.

"The trailer was totally dry, and it was so high off the ground, the car did not rot out underneath," Katerba said. "There was

no lock on the trailer — anybody could have walked up and opened it, but nobody messed with it. This was luck. That's all it was."

The old Ford's front brakes had locked up, but with a flatbed and a winch, the Ford was carefully coaxed out of the trailer it had been stored in for 37 years. Once the Ford was exposed to day light again, Katerba found it to be in good condition.

"The wagon is all original right down to the original finish on the wood, which is peeling now," he said. "Even the date of

"The '48 is great and I love original cars. I would rather leave the scratched paint in place."

manufacture is still visible on the firewall, dated in a yellow factory stamping from Feb. 25, 1948. Only a light coating of rust is visible on the underside of the floor pan with the paint still visible underneath."

But after 61 years, the Ford is not without a few faults.

"There are some issues," Katerba said. "There is some minor damage to the passenger quarter panel and the rear mahogany tailgate panels need replacing, along with the rear window frame. It's not bad, though, for not seeing sunlight for 37 years."

Since retrieving the Ford in April, Katerba has quickly grown excited about the advantages driving the 1948 Ford will offer over the 1939 Plymouth woodie.

"The Ford has a V-8 versus a flathead six," Katerba said. "It's a longer, bigger car. The rear windows crank down. They are not sliders, like on the '39 Plymouth.

Katerba plans to keep the 1948 Ford woodie a nice original, down to the paint, but he acknowledges some exterior work will have to be done to make it roadworthy.

"The '48 is great and I love original cars.

I would rather leave the scratched paint in place. The '48 is pretty nice — it's had some things done to it, but nothing major. I was missing a couple pieces of wood, and I am getting help from [famous woodie collector] Nick Alexander. I've had several conversations with him and he's very willing to help, and he's knowledgeable about these cars. The man is a true hobbyist. He has already helped me locate an NOS upper and lower tailgate and a quarter panel to make the Ford's body complete. Nick's shop manager, Jamie Torres, has also helped with technical questions."

Mechanically, Katerba has freed the brakes and pulled the flathead V-8 for a rebuild. Unfortunately, the original block was cracked and he's searching for a good 59AB block. Perhaps in 2010, the woodie will be rolling down the road again.

For now, two woodies, one unloved and both forgotten, share a home again. This time, their digs are a little more homey than a nearly forgotten semi trailer in a farm field.

By Angelo Van Bogart

CHEVROLET DREAM CAR'S PIECES COME BACK TOGETHER

The 1955 Biscayne as it appeared when Joe Bortz first saw it at Warhoop's Used Auto and Truck Parts in 1989. The car is seen in its cut-up state with the doors and roof severed, but the lower half was uncut. (Joe Bortz photo)

Resurrecting the 1955 Chevrolet Biscayne show car isn't quite like Johnny Cash's song about assembling a Cadillac with parts from the assembly line; it's more like assembling a 1,000-piece puzzle with many of its pieces missing.

Since saving the tattered and scattered remains of the ex-General Motors show car more than a decade ago from dream car goldmine Warhoop's Used Auto and Truck Parts in Warren, Michigan, owner Joe Bortz and his restoration team have completed significant amounts of work to the body of the Biscayne.

"When I (first) saw the Biscayne, it was just a body with no doors on it," Bortz said. "The roof was laying inside the car and the doors were inside the car. It was just a total

The reassembled body of the Biscayne. Parts of the original light metallic green paint are still visible on the car. (Joe Bortz photo)

wreck. If you would have looked at it, you would have said there's no way anybody is going to salvage this.

"It was just piled up, laying on top of a bunch of cars in a corner (of the yard) where you couldn't see it." But after years of work, the Biscayne's future is looking much brighter.

"The body really looks terrific, and we are preparing a chassis for this project, which we expect to have finished by the summer of 2004," Bortz said.

Even though the Biscayne had seen little or no road action, Bortz' crew had to dedicate a significant amount of work to its body, because the car had been cut into 10 pieces

by yard owner Harry Warhoop, Sr. to fulfill GM's mandate that the car be destroyed shortly after arriving at his yard. After cutting the Biscayne into pieces, Warhoop's scattered its various body sections throughout the yard, often hiding parts in other vehicles rusting away on the property.

"The story goes that two days before Christmas, they (General Motors) sent one of their people to Warhoop's with two of the cars, the LaSalle II roadster and the Biscayne," Bortz related. "They were smart enough not to send the car over to the junkyard and say, 'Crush this car.' They sent one of their people to give witness to the cutting of the car and then the crushing."

"It was just piled up, laying on top of a bunch of cars in a corner (of the yard) where you couldn't see it."

"The guy was supposed to sit there and watch them (the show cars) get cut and then crushed. So they took the cars, the LaSalle II and the Biscayne, and they cut them. They cut the doors off, the roof off (of the cars)." Having witnessed the cutting of the cars, the GM representative said, " 'I know you guys will do it. Just put it in the crusher. I want to get home,'" Bortz said. When the GM representative left, Harry Warhoop, Sr. took the pieces and hid them, knowing he was preserving history for the future.

"The next day, the day before Christmas Eve, they (GM) brought in the other two cars, the LaSalle II sedan and the '56 Caddy Eldorado Brougham Town Car, and he (the GM representative) said, 'I can't wait around for you guys to cut them up. Just cut 'em up, crush 'em, and I'll just mark down that I saw everything.' So they took these two cars complete and hid them." This story explains why Bortz found the LaSalle II roadster and the Biscayne cut into pieces, but mostly complete, and both the Eldorado Brougham Town Car and LaSalle II sedan complete and uncut. When Warhoop's eventually offered the cars to Bortz, he purchased all four of them.

GM may have originally trusted War-hoop's to crush the cars, but instead War-hoop's wound up helping preserve the past.

In a November 23, 1989, *Old Cars Weekly* article that appeared shortly after Bortz found the cars, Bortz said that while the cars were cut apart, their dismemberment by Warhoop's had been carefully done so as to keep their components from being destroyed.

"They (the parts) were cut up and distributed throughout the yard," Bortz said in that 1989 article. "One (Warhoop's) employee found the top of the Biscayne in a panel truck. It was like getting a Renwal model car kit, but it was a real car."

Warhoop's was so careful in keeping parts of the show cars they had disassembled so many years earlier that when it came time to dig out a chrome generator for one of the LaSalle II's Bortz had bought, Harry Warhoop, Sr. remembered, after some careful thought, that it had been stashed behind a rafter in his shop.

When found, the Biscayne lacked a chassis, so Bortz' restoration crew constructed a new chassis from a production 1955 Chevrolet frame.

"The chassis is a '55 Chevy chassis at the front and then it narrows down to ac-

Chevrolet Biscayne Four-Door Hardtop Sedan

The 1955 Biscayne show car as it appeared before the public at Motorama displays throughout the country. Dream car collector Joe Bortz considers this car to be a "beautiful Level 1" dream car, because it is a completely original, one-of-a-kind show car sharing no body components with production cars.

The Biscayne looking more like it did in 1955.

"We worked on it for a couple of years and got the whole body together, so it is now ready to drop on a chassis."

commodate this body," Bortz said. "Right now, we're in the process of taking the '55 Chevy chassis and making it fit the rest of the body, and then we can start the restoration of it." Unlike the rear, the front of the production frame will require little, if any, modification.

"Internationally known rod and custom fabricator Kerry Hopperstead is making up the chassis, and after that, we'll get into the actual restoration." A correct-for-1955

small-block 265-cid V-8 and Powerglide transmission will get matched to the chassis, just as Chevrolet had fit into the Biscayne's engine bay, before its expected summer 2004 completion.

Right now, Bortz has the fiber glass-bodied Biscayne's body to the point where the doors swing open and the roof is back on.

"We worked on it for a couple of years and got the whole body together, so it is now ready to drop on a chassis," Bortz said.

Bortz also has the original windshield for the car, but it's cracked beyond repair. It will, however, be able to provide a template for a new piece of glass.

The car is "amazingly complete, but there are always things you have to make," Bortz said. "That's just part of getting into these really, really high-tech, high-dollar-cost restorations."

Because it had been dissected, the Biscayne will have its share of parts that will need to be handmade. "There were a few trim parts missing that we're going to have to make, but a lot of the important trim pieces, like the trim on the front and the headlight bezels, were still on the car." Some of those parts will be made in-house, but sometimes they are farmed out to fabricators or done in collaboration with Bortz's team and outside fabricators. Such restoration tasks require time.

"Bortz enjoys sharing his collection. The last time his cavalcade of dream cars toured venues throughout the United States was in the early 1990s, but right now he's more concerned with finding a permanent home for his collection in a museum or large mall where the public can see the cars.

He's also not done looking for retired dream cars. The latest addition to his collection is the acquisition of the 1961 Pontiac Monte Carlo, an open two-seater based on a shortened-chassis Tempest with a wrap-around cockpit windscreen. Like so many other Motorama dream cars, the Monte Carlo had found itself in good hands.

While he has sizeable collection, Bortz' quest for other dream cars continues. If you have information about a dream car, call Bortz at 847-668-2004.

Story update

As of 2009, a new chassis had been built for the 1955 Chevrolet Biscayne and custom glass had finally been fit to the body after much trial and error. Also, the car can be driven under its own power. As with any hand-built, one-of-a-kind vehicle, progress is slow, but Bortz is dedicated to seeing the car to completion.

By Brian Earnest

RED, WILLING & ABLE

'55 Ford country sedan is hard not to love

Doc Kirby's 1955 Ford Country Sedan has turned out to be an unlikely attention getter after sitting idle for 18 years.

D.L. "Doc" Kirby probably never figured his 1957 Chevrolet Nomad hot rod would get upstaged regularly by some mom and pop 1955 Ford wagon that happened to share the same garage After all, how exciting can a ho-hum — well, except for the bright red paint — eight-passenger, solid color, nothing special Happy Days hauler really be?

But Kirby's '55 Country Sedan is one of those cars that gets cooler the more you learn about it. From its unique solid color, to its low build numbers, to its interesting life story, this Ford station wagon is a true sleeper and great hobby car — one that Kirby and his wife can not only score with at shows and cruises, but also drive regularly as a part-time everyday car.

You could squeeze eight passengers in the Country Sedan with the third seat up, or flop both rear seat rows down and have yourself a nice cargo hauler.

For a car that was once largely neglected and sat untouched for 18 years, this old Ford is living a very happy second life.

"It gets a lot of looks and that's always fun when you're going up and down the highway and you get a thumbs-up from somebody," said Kirby, a resident of Mission Viejo, Calif. "You don't see these very often. You see the Ranch Wagons, but not these. I've always felt, 'Wow, you could really have some fun with that car.' My wife is crazy about it, too, so that helps. We named it Rosie to give it some personality."

Kirby has owned the car since 2006, but he has known about the car since it left the dealership lot 54 years ago. The car was originally purchased by the grandfather of one of Kirby's friends. "Bob (Kirby's friend) actually remembers riding in the third row seat on the way back from the dealership, and how great that felt," Kirby said.

The original owner had the car for many years before it wound up with his grandson. The car eventually went into storage, but Kirby never forgot about it. "It was stored out east of San Diego and basically just sat and sat, and the mice and rats were all in it …" he said.

Kirby finally convinced his friend to sell him the old wagon, and quickly commenced a gentle restoration that included rebuilding the car's original 272-cubic inch overhead-valve V-8 and Ford-omatic transmission. Kirby only replaced what he had to, however, and has stuck to his plan to keep the car as original as possible.

The Ford had sat with a mattress and box spring resting on its roof, but aside from some varmint damage, was still in pretty good shape. "The mattress was kind of funny because the mice had taken the stuffing out and made nests all over the car," Kirby said. "The tires were flat, the wiring was chewed

up, the lines were clogged ... and we had to replace the brakes to make it driveable, but it really didn't take that much to get it running. We kind of took it from there.

"Everything was there, so to speak, when we bought it and I just kept working on, kept working on it, kept working on it. We rebuilt the transmission, replaced some of the chrome ... The interior is pretty much original, but I did have to replace the headliner and sun visors. The car was repainted in about 1976, but it still has a very original type lead-based paint.

"I'm pretty anal about a lot of little things, but I wanted it to stay as original

and close to stock as possible. It has some scratches in it here and there. It has a very daily use look to it, and that's kind of been the whole idea."

Kirby has known about the car almost from the beginning of its life, but he believes one of his relatives might have seen it even earlier — before it even left the assembly line at the old Long Beach Ford plant. "I had an uncle that worked there. He was an inspector … They had a fire (at the Dearborn, Mich. records office) and all their records were destroyed, but the odds are that he was actually the one that inspected the car at the time it was built."

Kirby has done plenty of homework on the car and has accumulated lots of documentation, including a letter from his friend about the car's history. He notes that of the 47,320 V-8 Country Sedans built for 1955, not many had the single-color paint job. He says not many station wagons were built that year at Long Beach, and solid-color wagon were particularly scarce at that plant.

The Country Sedan was one notch below the Country Squire on the Ford wagon hierarchy during the 1950s and was identifiable in '55 by the dipping Fairlane sedan trim with "Country Sedan" on the rear fenders. All five Ford wagon were available with ei-

ther sixes or the new V-8s that year. The V-8s cost about $100 more.

The two-tone red-and-white interior is still in splendid condition on Kirby's car, and the wagon's unique third-row seat is a great conversation piece at car buff gatherings. " I always had station wagon envy as a kid," Kirby laughs. "I was an only child and seemed to always be stuck in the back seat of some kind of coupe. I'd see other families in their stations wagons, and it always looked like so much fun!"

The retired Kirby says he has taken his fetching Country Sedan to three shows and taken home awards each time. "We're un-defeated so far," he said. "People are curious about what we think it's worth. With a '57 Chevy or another car, you kind of know what it's worth or you can figure it out. But this one is so unusual …"

The odometer on the car reads 96,100 miles. Kirby figures he's put less than 1,000 miles on since getting the car back on the road, but there are sure to be many more miles in the future.

"We're kind of in between cars now, so I'll probably be driving it a little more on the weekends," he said. "It's certainly not a trailer queen, that's for sure."

Story and photos by Angelo Van Bogart

WIND WHISTLES THROUGH IMPERIAL CONVERTIBLE

Hiding in the woods near the *Old Cars Weekly* office in central Wisconsin was this 1956 Imperial convertible. Chrysler didn't build an Imperial convertible from 1952 to 1956, so this car's history is shrouded in mystery.

The bitter winter Wisconsin wind blows cold against the metal of a car that doesn't exist in Chrysler reference books. The car, a 1956 Imperial convertible, is protected only by an old truck bed topper that shields the car's convertible top and dirty white leather interior.

Blanketed by eight inches of March snow just a few miles from the Old Cars Weekly office rests this unusual Imperial with a partially known history. Despite being so close to this magazine's headquarters for nearly as long as the magazine has served hobbyists, the car eluded staff members until only a few years ago when a coworker mentioned that one of the cars on her family's property

The convertible top is barely visible through the windows on the truck bed cover employed to protect the roof of the car. The cover has done a good job of keeping the top and white leather interior intact.

was this '56 Imperial convertible.

I'd been to her home on several occasions, but I did not know about the old cars outside of her family's barn. I told her Chrysler didn't build Imperial convertibles in 1956, but the coworker knows her cars, so I had to check out this treasure hiding in the woods around her home.

On a fall day, several OCW staff members drove to the woods hiding the car with our escort. We walked past the barn and up the hill behind it. Once we crossed its crest, the back side of the hill revealed a trove of old cars: a 1975 Thunderbird, a Rambler station wagon, and a circa-1970 Chrysler

two-door hardtop, and many others. I can't tell you the exact years of all the aforementioned cars, because it wasn't those cars I was interested in. It was the Imperial convertible that grabbed my attention.

Examining the car immediately revealed that being parked in a field outside Iola, Wisconsin, since the early 1970s has not been kind to the Imperial's metal. Its "gunsight" taillights are snapped off at their bases, and most of the front clip is gone, though the hood is still present and is acting as a lean-to over the Hemi engine. The Hemi's valve covers are covered with a patina of rust, and a nest of twigs and needles

The Imperial has sunk up to its rocker panels, and in this view, the lack of a passenger front fender is evident.

in the intake manifold prove that the engine compartment has been the home for forest creatures for several years. The car has sunk into the earth up to its rocker panels, making it a true buried treasure for anyone who rescues it, whether it's the current owner or a future hobbyists, if it can even be saved.

Our escort, who took us to the giant X where the treasure was hidden, told me that her family did not own the car, but had been storing it on their property for the past 30 years for a friend. After the staff assessed the car and determined that it was, indeed, a 1956 Imperial convertible, and that the work to make the car a convertible was too well done to be a backyard conversion, I wrote down the owner's phone number so I could contact him. I needed to learn more about his car.

I learned Bob, the owner, knew what he had hiding in the woods north of his home. He knew Chrysler didn't offer Imperial convertibles that year, at least in their catalog, but he said that he was told his '56 Imperial convertible and a second similar car were, indeed, built by Chrysler Corp. He then shared what he knew of his car's history.

"This car was built for someone that owned a tannery in Chicago," Bob said. "He had got it for his wife. He had really strong

One Imperial convertible was built in 1955, but it wasn't built for just anybody; it was built for K.T. Keller, Chrysler Corp.'s chairman of the board. No other Imperial convertibles are known to have been built by Chrysler Corp. from 1952 to 1956.

connections at Chrysler."

Bob's father-in-law was a supplier to the tannery, and the tannery owner knew he was a car fanatic, especially for Chryslers, so when his wife was done with the car, he offered it to Bob's father-in-law in the 1960s.

Sometime after that, Bob's father-in-law was driving the Imperial along Wisconsin's I-43 on a foggy night and he was the last person in a chain-reaction accident. Luckily, no one followed him into the pile-up, and only the front of the car was damaged.

Bob's father-in-law looked into repairing the car, but then gave it to Bob in damaged condition. Bob got as far as tossing out the damaged front fender and grille, and then the car went into storage. The car bounced around from storage building to building, and eventually to the outskirts of Iola three decades ago.

"I was going to restore it, but I never got around to it," Bob said, adding that the car's outdoor resting place was only intended to be temporary. "When I put it back there, there were no trees." Now, there's a forest around the car.

Another piece of the puzzle comes from the dealership tag on the back of the

"When I put it back there, there were no trees." Now, there's a forest around the car.

car that shows, at some point, the car went through Rank & Son, a Milwaukee dealership that sold Dodges in the 1950s. Wally Rank was president of the Milwaukee dealership, which now sells Buicks, Pontiacs, and GMCs. Rank was also a well-known car collector who had many interesting cars in his collection, including Classic-era cars and the 1958 Buick Wells Fargo convertible. When the Imperial passed through the dealership is unknown.

The Imperial's vehicle identification number, located on a tag fastened with phillips screws to the door sill, was submitted to the Walter P. Chrysler Museum in an attempt to learn the mysterious car's history. The museum determined the car is a Detroit-built Newport assembled near the end of 1956 model year production.

The fact that the car was identified as a Newport by the VIN points to the notion that the car was transformed into an Imperial sometime after it was christened as a Newport on the assembly line. Now the only question is when the conversion was done. Since the basic sheet metal from the cowl to the rear fenders is shared between the Imperial and Chryslers, this would not have been a difficult alteration. Since the car is known to have been an Imperial since at least the 1960s, and its weathered black paint appears to be original, it seems likely the car was made into an Imperial very early, if not by Chrysler Corp.

If this car was built by the Chrysler Corp., it would not be the only mid-1950s Imperial convertible built, despite the fact the model was not offered to the public from 1952 to 1956. A beautifully restored emerald green 1955 Imperial convertible built for Chrysler Corp. Chairman of the Board K.T. Keller exists and was displayed at Hershey in 2001. However, that car features a serial number with an engineering experimental code 9999, whereas this 1956 has a New Yorker VIN, as well as many unique features not found on any other Imperial or other Chrysler product of the time.

Whether the presence of the '55 Imperial convertible built for Keller leads credence to the history of this 1956 Imperial convertible is as debatable as the builder of the car itself.

Story and photos by Angelo Van Bogart

CAR BUFFS RESPOND TO IMPERIAL MYSTERY

The wheelbase measures 126 inches on this mystery car, which is consistent with the other New Yorker-based 1956 Imperial convertibles known to have been built for Chrysler Corp. Production Imperial two-door hardtops carried longer 133-inch wheelbases.

Following the X on a treasure map to the pot of gold is only half of the fun. Learning how the treasure came to be is the other half, especially when you can confirm that the treasure chest isn't full of fool's gold.

When a story on a 1956 Imperial convertible appeared in the March 3, 2005, issue of *Old Cars Weekly*, several readers wrote in.

Many wanted to know where this piece of Chrysler Corp. history was and how much it would cost to buy the car and drag it from its long slumber in the central Wisconsin woods where it has rested for more than 30 years. But, several people were also able to offer some clues to the origins of the 1956 Imperial convertibles, and one could even

The March 3, 2005, issue of Old Cars Weekly pictured this 1956 Imperial convertible hidden in some Wisconsin woods. From the known facts cited in the initial story, several readers could verify that this car was one of only a few 1956 Imperical convertibles built for Chrysler that year.

remember seeing the car in the 1950s. All of the correspondence proved that the car was, indeed, a New Yorker-based Imperial convertible built for Chrysler Corp. And it wasn't the only one.

Reader Allen Radtke remembers seeing the Imperial when it was new, or nearly new. In 1956-'57, Radtke worked in River Hills, Wisconsin, a suburb of Milwaukee, trimming trees during the summer.

"I believe it was in '56 that I worked on an estate in the 700 W. Greentree Rd. area and saw a 1956 Imperial convertible that was black," Radtke wrote. "The gentleman of the house bought the car for his wife. This was where I trimmed for three to four

"At the time, the owner said it was one-of-a-kind, and he was very proud to get it for his wife."

"... I thought there were only two made, but now, adding in the one in Wisconsin, I know the whereabouts of three such cars."

weeks and saw this magnificant auto parked and driven with the top down most of the time. At the time, the owner said it was one-of-a-kind, and he was very proud to get it for his wife. And she looked well driving it. My memory doesn't serve me very well as I did other jobs in the area, but I thought their name was Lindstrum. I'm not sure. I am sure about the car and its year, model, and color."

Another reader even wrote to say that Bob, the owner of the Imperial, had shown him the car several years ago, and "that it looks pretty much the same as when he showed it to me 20 years ago."

Other readers wrote to say that there are other legitimate 1956 Imperial convertibles, and though no one can pinpoint exactly how many were built, it is believed that no more than four were constructed.

All of the cars, including the Imperial in Winsconsin, are based on New Yorker convertibles, were built late in the year, and have New Yorker lion emblems in the instrument cluster.

Chip Loree, owner of the 1955 Imperial convertible pictured with the 1956 Imperial story in the March 3, 2005, issue, said that in researching the history of his car, he became aware of a "few" 1956 Imperial convertibles. "Until your article, I thought there were only two made, but now, adding in the one in Wisconsin, I know the whereabouts of three such cars," Loree wrote.

The 1955 Imperial convertible

For a little background information on mid-1950s Imperial convertibles, Loree shared the story of his car, which was built for Chrsler Corp. Chariman of the Board K.T. Keller.

"Even though K.T. Keller had the reputation of being a very conservative leader who put functionality above all in his automobile 'top ten,' K.T. always felt that, from a marketing standpoint, Chrysler's finest car, the Imperial, should be available in the flashiest of body styles, the convertible," Loree wrote.

Sales were never very impressive for

Imperial convertibles, and Loree suspected that from a money-making standpoint, the Imperial convertibles were a "dismal failure" in the years they were offered. But he also pointed out that Chrysler realized the image-building importance of marketing a convertible, and did so, regardles of sales history, at interesting times in the company's history. The 1937 and '38 Imperial convertibles came after the "Airflow disaster," and again with the introduction of the Hemi engine in 1951. "Certainly, one would think the former was out of perceived necessity, and the latter was designed to take full advantage of the biggest

mechanical innovation to be introduced in a production automobile in many, many years," Loree said.

"The desire to include this flashy automotive jewel as the marketing focal point for the Corporation never left K. T.'s mind. Even when brilliant designer Virgil Exner completely revamped all of Chrysler Corp.'s product lines with his 'Hundred Million Dollar Look' in 1955, an Imperial convertible remained down the list of priorities for everyone except K.T. Keller!

"K.T. decided that the only way he was going to get his elusive Imperial convertible was to build one himself. With the unlimited resources of Chrysler Central Engineering, the design talents of Ghia of Turin, Italy, and the wonderful automotive mind of K.T. himself, one of the most significant postwar automobiles was created over the next nine months."

Loree has obtained accounts from Ray Schafer, Burt Dickinson, and Bill Smith, who were all engineers who built the 1955 Imperial convertible for Keller.

Schafer told Loree, "It was a very special situation, building a car for the chairman. You never wanted to do anything that you would be ashamed of. Keller would ask if we could do this or that, and, of course, we would never say no. With all the facilities at our beck and call, we really could do almost anything."

Following the completion of his Imperial convertible, Keller took his new convertible to the exclusive Detroit Athletic Club (DAC) on several occasions, according to Loree.

"It was at the DAC that KT's buddies admired his convertible, and pressured him to have more made," Loree wrote. "The Keller car is a true prototype; it has hundreds of model shop castings and one-off parts that would make it prohibitive to reproduce. Apparently the desire to drive a car similar to the Keller car continued to get attention in the inner circles of Chrysler Corp. In 1956, Chrysler sent a number (maybe three) of New Yorker convertibles to well-known car customizer George Bar-

ris to perform the transformation into an Imperial. One such car is in Sacramento, California. It was built for Mr. Paul Smith, who was the editor in chief of *Collier's* magazine, and a known car buff. Like the owner of the tannery in Chicago you mention in your article, Smith reportedly had close ties with the upper echelon at Chrysler. Another such car still exists and currently is in Massachussetts, although it is on the brink of non-existence. This car previously resided in Ohio for many years and was originally built for E. C. Quinn, president of the Chrysler division."

From New Yorker to Imperial

Loree inspected the Sacramento car and learned that to convert the New Yorker into an Imperial, only very simple modifications of bolt-on parts were required.

"As is the case with the Wisconsin car, the California car and the Massachussetts car have New Yorker VINs. The Chrysler Historical Collection has no real detail on how they were converted. One detail in the conversion was left undone: the New Yorker lion still remains between the instrument clusters." The car in question does, indeed, still have its New Yorker lion in the proper location.

A friend of Loree's who has been a Chrysler historian all his life insisted that there were three uniquely made Imperial convertibles from that era. Loree initially thought that that number included his 1955,

but now he believes that his friend meant that there were three 1956 Imperial convertibles in addition to the 1955 Imperial convertible built for K.T. Keller.

Worrell Stout remembered reading an article about mid-1950s Imperial convertibles in this or another publication several years ago that told of Keller's 1955 convertible and of a matched pair of '56 Imperial convertibles also bult for some other important Chrysler figure and his wife.

"The 1956s were built very late in the year and came with 392 engines and Torqueflite transmissions," Stout said. Since the Imperial convertible in question has a late serial number, Stout's comments support the idea

that the Wisconsin Imperial is one of the convertibles built for the corporation.

"I seem to remember that at least one of the '56s was pink. I don't recall the colors of all three. I think at least one was built for K.T. Keller. All three were in the hands of collectors at the time of the article, and all three were either excellent or restored. I don't beleive the Wisconsin car is one of the three, so we might possibly have an unknown number four here."

Building a 1956 Imperial

Automotive historian Kit Foster did some research on his own and determined that Imperials had their own 133-inch wheelbase, as compared to the 126-inch wheelbase of the Chryslers. When measured, the Wisconsin Imperial was found to have a 126-inch wheelbase, which would be consistent with the other known New Yorker-based 1956 Imperial convertibles.

In looking in an interchange manual, Foster also learned that an Imperial front clip bolts to a New Yorker (a la Chrysler 300B). The additional length in the Imperial body was found behind the passenger compartment between the roof and the trunk lid, so the rear fenders from an Imperial would not simply fit onto a New Yorker like the Imperial front end would. This is consistent with Loree's assessment that the rear Imperial-only parts, namely, the rear fender extensions, were bolted onto New Yorker convertibles to make the three or four Imperial convertibles.

The fate of the Wisconsin Imperial

Following the appearance of the story about his car in *Old Cars Weekly*, the owner was able to explain one last clue on his car, the Rank & Son dealership tag below the trunklid. Bob said that the connection with Wally Rank "wasn't significant regarding the history of the car, but he did know a lot of the details," Bob said.

"My mother-in-law was his private secretary for many years, and she was the behind-the-scenes organizer for all of the car shows that were held at Rank & Son Buick on Green Bay Ave. in Milwaukee. My father-in-law and Wally were very close friends and were fellow members of one or more Wisconsin antique car collector clubs. I believe the Rank & Son sticker was only on the car as a favor, because Wally's restoration people and his dealership did all the work on the car."

In June 2007, Bob's friend retrieved the Imperial convertible from its outdoor resting place and moved it to an indoor storage facility. Unfortunately, it still awaits restoration with no time line for its rejuvenation.

There's no telling what's in store for this rare machine, but hopefully, it will be retrieved from its long slumber and made to look like the treasure it was and could be again.

Story and photos by Brian Earnest

FACTORY FRESH

Olds fan finds a truly 'Super' 88 hiding in the Wisconsin cheese

Ed Servais acted fast when a friend told him about a low-mileage 1958 Oldsmobile that was for sale. The neglected car hadn't been started in more than 30 years, but within a month, Servais had it back on the road. Eleven years later, he's still driving his beautiful blue-and-white Super 88.

"**B**arn find" is a familiar, and some might argue slightly overused, term when it comes to the old car hobby. It's thrown around as a catch-all description for cars that get uncovered in the strangest of places, including actual barns, sheds, chicken coups and various other agrarian structures. It also loosely applies to vehicles that might turn up in warehouses, storage facilities, under garage tarps or even sealed semi trailers.

But a "cheese factory" find? Well, that could probably only happen in Wisconsin, where, next to beer, bratwurst and the Green Bay Packers, cheese is king.

Ed Servais of De Pere, Wis., might well have the only "cheese factory" tale to tell in old car circles, and he has a shiny, almost

The interior of the '58 Oldsmobile is like the rest of the car — all original.

all-original 1958 Oldsmobile Super 88 four-door Holiday hardtop to prove his story.

"Yeah, it's quite an unusual story, I guess," Servais admits with a chuckle.

Servais was already a bit of an Oldsmobile fan 11 years ago when he got a call from a buddy about a car. Servais owned a 1949 Olds 88 coupe and earlier had a 1950 Olds Holiday, but he wasn't exactly shopping for another car when his phone rang.

"My friend had been doing some contracting work at this cheese factory, and he heard about the car and gave me a call, because he knew I liked Oldsmobiles," Servais recalled. "It belonged to the original owner of the cheese factory. One day it wouldn't

start, so the workers there, they were going to jumpstart it and they hooked a 24-volt jumpstarter that they used on the big trucks, and they burned up all the wiring, blew up the battery and burnt up the regulator and everything. They burned everything up through the fuse box, and they unhooked that just in time or I think the whole car would have burned up … So then they just parked it."

And the car stayed parked at the facility for more than three decades. During that time, the original owner died and the car sat untouched until it was finally deemed a nuisance to even have around, even though it had less than 40,000 miles on the odometer.

The Super 88 shared its 371-cid, 305-hp engine with its bigger sibling, the 98.

"One day, the owner of the cheese factory, who was the grandson of the original owner of the car, saw his guys pushing the car by hand, and he said, 'I can't afford to pay you guys to push this car around, so get rid of that car.' My friend let me know about it one weekend … and by Tuesday morning I was getting it on my trailer," Servais laughed. "What I can't understand is that the grandson didn't have much feeling for the car. I mean, if it was my grandpa's car, I don't care what the story was, it would never get sold, but he just wanted it out of there!"

The car needed all new wiring and electricals, and Servais obviously couldn't turn the engine over, but the Olds simply looked too good to pass up. Not long after he got the car home and got a good look at the paint, chrome and interior, he knew he had made a good gamble.

"Of course, I didn't hear it run, so the transmission could have been bad, or engine could have been bad, but it fired up and it ran just beautiful. It drove beautiful," he said. "I was able to order a complete wiring harness for everything under the hood and everything under the dash, and in about three weeks time, I had it all wired, and when I drove it out of my driveway, which was in 1998, it turned over 40,000 miles."

The Super 88 Series was Oldsmobile's

mid-range offering for 1958, placed between the low-end Dynamic 88 lineup and the high-end 98 series. The Super 88s shared a 122.5-inch wheelbase with the Dynamics and the popular, overhead-valve 371-cid/305-hp base engine with the 98s.

The Super 88s came in five body styles: two- and four-door Holidays (hardtops), four-door sedans, two-door convertibles and four-door wagons. With 27,521 produced for the model year, the four-door Holidays, like Servais' car, were the second-best sellers behind the four-door sedans (33,844).

While some criticize the looks of the '58 Oldsmobiles, they remain head-turners. With bold body-side trim and contours, and stylish grille, headlamp and tail lamp

assemblies, the Super 88 was a handsome package. And during the 1950s, Oldsmobile gave its cars a significant facelift nearly every year. The late-'50s cars, in particularly, each have their own distinctive designs.

Standard equipment for the '58 Super 88s included a padded dash, courtesy lights, special side moldings and chrome rocker panel moldings. The base price for the four-door hardtops was $3,339. Servais' car has a few additional add-ons, including the optional Jetaway transmission, power steering and brakes, speed sensor and signal-seeking radio with foot switch.

Aside from the new wiring, the only thing on Servais' car that isn't original equipment is the alternator, which replaced

"It handles and drives really nice. It's just a beautiful car."

the factory generator. "It's a driver. I drive it all the time," he said. "Last year I went to the Oldsmobile Nationals over in Deerborn, Mich., and I drove it over there. I got a plaque for the car being all-original, and they are pretty fussy over what they consider original. In that class there was like 39 cars, all Oldsmobiles, and when they got done looking at all of them, there were only about 18 left [judged as original], and mine was one of them."

The lovely Olds still wears its original Tropical Mist blue paint and factory white paint on the top. Everything in the interior is untouched. "It's never been painted, and I don't plan on painting it," Servais said. "It's not the best. It's got a few little nicks and scratches, but I'm going to leave it that way because they are only original once, I guess.

"I [considered restoring it] at first. I thought about having it painted, but it's a driver, and I could spend a lot of money on the car, but then I'd be afraid to drive it. It took 40 years for it to get its first 40,000 miles, and only 10 years to get its second 40,000. It's got over 80,000 miles on it now. We drive it, that's for sure.

"My wife always liked the '58s, but I didn't really like them that much until I got one, then I really began to like them. It handles and drives really nice. It's just a beautiful car."

BARN-FIND CONVERTIBLE: LAST CHRYSLER 300-F

**This 1960 Chrysler 300-F convertible was barn find in Connecticut.
In addition to being an already-desirable 300-F convertible, it is also the last 300-F built.**

It is the dream of many vintage automobile lovers to have the ultimate barn find — the car that had sat for decades due to a complicated estate situation or some other factor. The car that was completely forgotten about just waits for that lucky person to open the barn door and awaken it from years of slumber. It is fairly often that a car is discovered, although it seems that most of the "good ones" have long since been torn from the grasp of anonymity and are back on the road.

Connecticut, like most other states, can offer its share of barn finds. Rumors had

The black-and-white convertible is in factory-original condition. The 300-F was in a collection of "Letter Cars" for decades before becoming a part of the Schibley Collection in 2006.

I had personally searched for the car for more than two years and had no success, chasing one wrong lead after another.

circulated for years in and around Bridgeport that a 1960 Chrysler 300-F convertible sat untouched in someone's garage in neighboring Milford. I had personally searched for the car for more than two years and had no success, chasing one wrong lead after another.

One year ago, someone from one of the car clubs sent an e-mail indicating that a recently discovered 300-F convertible was now for sale — and it was in Bridgeport. Of course, I picked up the phone to discover that this was the lost 300-F convertible that had long been rumored. The Chrysler 300 Club International was notified; indeed, this was a brand-new find, and the club set up to doing what they will do for any member — a "work-up" for this car.

A work-up is a pretty simple process. Gil Cunningham is the club historian and has

The heart of the 300-F is the 413-cid V-8 producing 375 hp. The dual four-barrels use the long-ram induction system to feed the engine.

actual copies of the original micro-films that Chrysler produced in 1960. He looks up the serial number and some other data on the micro film and provides a report on the provenance of the car. When Gil did the work, he found out "Part Two" of this story was a stunning find: The car was the last 300F built by Chrysler. Among the rarest of the "Letter Cars," the 300-F convertible has stood the test of time like few other cars built in its day. Between the documents found in the car, and the work-up provided by the club, virtually all of the history became evident on this car.

Sold new in July of 1960 to Mr. Wallace Lines of Milford, this car was ordered from the factory as an extraordinarily optioned car. Among the options selected were two-zone air conditioning, tinted windows, upgraded radio, dual outside mirrors, power antenna and vacuum locks. According to the Chrysler 300 Club International records, this is one of the most highly optioned 300-Fs to leave the factory.

Mr. Lines would be the last person in the world to order and receive a 1960 Chrysler 300-F. With the completion of this very car, the factory would shut down for retooling to build the next iteration of Letter Cars, the 300-G. The very first 300-Gs would roll off

The original interior features leather upholstery and copious amounts of bright trim. The car is equipped with two-zone air conditioning and vacuum locks.

the line only a couple of weeks later.

Lines would enjoy the car for three years and then sell it on Dec. 20, 1965, to the second owner, Henry DeSiena of Stratford, Conn., one town away from Milford. DeSiena was an early Letter-Car collector and added this car to a growing collection of Letter Cars that would stay hidden away for nearly 40 years. This 300-F went to the Schibley Collection in mid 2006 and has stayed there since.

The car still carries its original 413-cid engine generating 375 hp. It is coupled to the venerable cast-iron TorqueFlite three-speed automatic transmission and has dual four-barrel carburetors with the long-ram induction system.

The Worldwide Group will be offering this car in running, as-found condition at the Houston Classic Auction on May 5, 2007, along with the rest of the Schibley Letter-Car collection. More information on this car, including photographs, can be found at www.WWGauctions.com.

Story by Angelo Van Bogart
Photos by Bob Brown and George Collar

FOUND: IOWA 'LETTER CAR' STASH

Finned-car collectors find a pair of 300 ragtops, and more

A proud George Collar stands next to 1960 300-F and 1961 300-G convertibles.
The dusty ragtops are pictured in the cinder-block garage where they were found.
Several of the cars wear license plates last renewed in 1967.

With interest and values of Chrysler "Letter Cars" growing with nearly every passing year, the first place you'd expect to see a 1960 Chrysler 300-F or 300-G is at a car show. The last place is the "bad

part" of Davenport, Iowa, behind an olive green two-story slated for destruction.

George Collar and Bob Brown of Wisconsin Rapids, Wis., had decided that, because of the quickly escalating values

The 1949 Lincoln Cosmopolitan coupe and 1955 Chrysler
C-300 were also part of the Davenport, Iowa, car stash.

of finned MoPars, they would not add any 1950s or '60s Chryslers to their already sizable collection. The decision was agreed upon, despite the fact they still didn't own the current king of "Letter Cars" — a 1960 300-F convertible — a MoPar they had wanted for several years. That plan was quickly reversed, however, when fellow finned MoPar fan Dr. Milt McMillen contacted them in 2008.

McMillen spotted an innocuous advertisement on a Chryser Web site simply stating "Chrysler 300s for sale." Upon further investigation, He learned that a long-deceased enthusiast's car collection was for sale, and that it included some intriguing 1950s and early-1960s cars, including a 1958 Plymouth Fury with dual quads, a 1963 Pontiac Catalina with a tri-power 421-cid V-8, a 1955 Chrysler C-300 and a pair of "Letter Car" convertibles: a 1960 300-F and a 1961 300-G.

McMillen knew that Brown and Collar wanted a 300-F convertible to match a 300-

Chrysler only built 1,212 Chrysler 300-F models in 1960, and of those, a scant 248 were convertibles.

After the deal was sealed, Collar and Brown loaded up the special-order Sheffield Silver 1961 Chrysler 300-G (background), white 1960 Chrysler 300-F (middle) and 1960 Chrysler New Yorker sedan (foreground) for the cars' new garage in Wisconsin Rapids, Wis.

F hardtop they already owned, and so he forwarded the information about the "Letter Cars."

After receiving the tip, Brown didn't waste any time getting in touch with the deceased owner's son. Chrysler only built 1,212 Chrysler 300-F models in 1960, and of those, a scant 248 were convert-

ibles. Given the demand for 300-F models, Brown knew time was of the essence. He called on a Saturday morning with a plan to see the cars the next day. After hanging up the phone, Brown discovered the cars were only about seven hours away from his Wisconsin Rapids home, so he and Collar jumped in a vehicle and drove to Davenport

Bob Brown (left), the seller (middle) and George Collar (right) stand with the loaded finned car fleet for their parade to Wisconsin. This 2008 sight was surely a neck-spinner in traffic as the caravan made its way from Iowa.

that day. When they arrived in Davenport, it was already dark, but Brown and Collar figured they would try to see the cars that night. They called the son to surprise him with news of their early arrival and to view the 300s that night.

Brown recalled, "When I called to say, 'We're here,' the son said, 'It's not possible to see the cars tonight. After dark, you hear gun shots.'

"We were concerned the evening we went there, that the whole thing was some kind of scam. After I talked to the guy, he was concerned it was a scam, too. He thought somebody was going to take him down there and shoot him. We laughed about it after we made the deal and they saw we were legiti-

mate and I saw they were legitimate."

The pair wisely held off until morning, and it was worth the wait. Behind the rough house were cinder-block garages that contained long-hidden cars last licensed no later than the early 1970s. Over time, the cars had sunk on their flat tires, making it impossible to see their condition underneath. It was also obvious that animals had found a way into the garage, but the cars were clearly complete, straight and solid. The condition of the 300-F convertible alone reflected that of a seven-year-old car that had been parked for 40 years.

"The widow told me they bought the '61 300-G convertible in Florida, which is confirmed with the dealer information we got

"We were concerned the evening we went there, that the whole thing was some kind of scam. After I talked to the guy, he was concerned it was a scam, too. He thought somebody was going to take him down there and shoot him."

from Chrysler archives and the title, and moved it to Iowa in the late 1960s or early '70s, she couldn't remember when," Brown said. "She did say they drove the 300-G convertible as a daily driver when it was in Florida."

Just as they hoped, Brown and Collar were able to make a deal with the owners on the 300-F convertible, a white example still retaining the factory-installed 413-cid wedge-head V-8 with dual four-barrel carburetors crowning a set of long-ram intake manifolds.

What Collar and Brown didn't expect was to be mesmerized by the 300-G convertible parked next to the 300-F. The convertible was only six years old when it was parked and, in addition to the same dual-carbureted 413-cid engine, it was equipped with air conditioning and a specially sprayed Sheffield Silver color — a hue not offered among the four color choices available on the 300-G

that year. For parts, a third Chrysler, a 1960 New Yorker sedan, was also purchased out of the Davenport collection.

The pair of collectors expect to give their new finds a proper restoration in the next few years. When the cars are completed, they hope to display the 300s with their other MoPars at the Iola Old Car Show.

And what about that good friend who led Collar and Brown to the 300s? He made off with the 1958 Fury. Not a bad deal all around.

Story update

Since the 1961 Chrysler 300-G convertible is the only such car known to be painted Sheffield Silver, it underwent restoration first. As of 2009, its restoration was rapidly progressing.

Once the 300-G is finished, Collar and Brown plan to begin restoration work on the 300-F convertible.

By Robert J. LeBlanc

OLDSMOBILE FREED FROM URBAN TOMB

I wasn't too excited when I learned about this 1960 Oldsmobile 88 sedan until I saw how pristine the original features of the low-mileage car remained. (Robert J. LeBlanc photo)

If you love old cars as much as I do, you probably have fantasies about finding an old car in a barn that hasn't been driven in years. Add to this dream the idea that the car's condition is so good, it looks as though it came through a time tunnel. "Impossible," you say? Not really — and it probably happens more often than you think.

Around the end of October, 1991, I received a call from an elderly woman about an old car that she wanted to sell. I asked for some information, including the year, condition, etc. When I learned the car was

"We had a little difficulty opening the doors, but once opened, I saw the car. At that point, I had to do all I could to hide my excitement, to put it mildly!"

a 1960 Olds 88 four-door sedan, and that it hadn't run since 1968, I wasn't too excited, but I made an appointment to look at the car.

Arriving at the address, I noticed that the house was empty and that a "for sale" sign was on the lawn. The lady informed me that the house originally belonged to her parents, and that she and her bachelor brother lived there until he passed away. Her brother was the owner of the car, but he became paralyzed in 1968, and the car was not used again. I received all of this information from her while standing in her driveway before I saw the car.

The house was located among others built around the turn of the century. The garage, or barn, was as old as the house, and because of the location, the windows were boarded up tight. The garage doors were barn-type sliders on rollers.

We had a little difficulty opening the doors, but once I opened them, I saw the car. At that point, I had to do all I could to hide my excitement, to put it mildly!

Realizing at first glance that this car was in showroom condition, I immediately headed for the driver's door to peak at the odometer, which showed only 11,114 miles. Checking the left front door, I found a service sticker dated Aug. 9, 1967, at 10,600 miles. Nothing had ever been changed or replaced, and it even still had the paper floor mats that the dealer put in to protect the floor coverings.

The gas tank was bone dry, which was to my advantage, since old gas usually gums up the system. The battery had frozen and split through the years, and it was the only part we had to replace to try to start the engine.

Before going any further, I realized that I should make an offer and try to close the deal. It took a few weeks and a little haggling, but a deal was made, and I became this car's second owner. When I returned to pick up the car with a friend, we arrived with a battery, five gallons of gas, and a toolbox. Our intention was to drive it home after we started it, and we almost made it.

First, we checked all of the levels in the oil, water, and transmission. We installed the battery, put the key in the ignition, crossed our fingers, and turned the key. The engine turned over, to our amazement, and after a few revolutions, I noticed that the oil pressure light went out. Next, we checked for spark, which proved to be very good. We put about three or four gallons of gas in the tank, and filled a couple of cups to pour into the carburetor. I put about four or five ounces of gas in the carb, we looked at each other for a second, and I turned the key. After about five or six revolutions, the engine fired up and purred like a kitten. We could have driven this car home, but the brake cylinders were sticking, so to be safe, it was towed.

I have been fooling with old cars for 35 years, and trying to figure out how this car survived in such good shape had me baffled, until I started to realize a few facts: The barn was dry and dark, and there were no windows or openings in the barn. The owners kept old cotton sheets over the entire car and had mothballs everywhere, and the barn was well shaded by buildings and trees, so there weren't any drastic changes in temperature inside.

So car buffs, keep looking — it could happen to you!

By Angelo Van Bogart

21 TRAILERS OF MUSCLE
The tale of Donald Schlag's historic hidden stash

Seeing the light of day for the first time in more than 25 years is this fuel-injected 1957 Corvette. This Corvette is among 14 cars found in 21 trailers housing high-performance Corvette and Chevrolet parts collected by a Green Bay, Wis., man over many years.

Larry Fisette had no idea whether he was buying King Tut's tomb or Al Capone's vault when he agreed to buy 21 trailers said to be full of Corvettes and Chevrolet muscle cars and parts. Luckily, all of the rumors he had heard whispered around his northeast

Wisconsin home turned out to be more true than he ever dreamed.

Fisette, a De Pere, Wis., restorer and automotive repair shop proprietor, opened trailers one-by-one and found a Yenko Camaro with 45,000 miles; a pair of low-mile-

Larry Fisette (top right) and a few of his helpers unload an LS-6 454-cid engine with a four-speed bellhousing from a trailer. The trailers contained 150 muscle car engines.

The only car Donald Schlag is known to have sold is this fuel-injected Corvette, shown packed from one of his annual parts-hunting trips to California. The day after he sold the car, the new buyer totalled it.

Donald Schlag is pictured with one of his 1957 Corvettes in this early photo. This car was found painted black in one of the trailers.

The Yenko Camaro that Schlag squirreled away was wedged between a 1967 Camaro SS/RS and a dune buggy in one of 21 trailers full of parts.

age 1970 LS-6 Chevelles; a 1972 Camaro Z/28; two 1957 Corvettes, one a fuel-injected car, the other a dual-four-barrel-equipped example; and several other Chevrolet performance cars. Filling in the space around the cars like water around pebbles was an inventory of NOS and used performance parts that would make a Nickey Chevrolet parts manager jealous.

How the trailers came to be full of new Corvette side exhaust systems, factory Corvette race parts, and highly desirable engines and parts is as interesting as the man who filled them.

The late Donald Schlag's passion for Chevrolet performance cars, even when they were new, gave him the foresight to realize that, someday, others would have just as much interest in these vehicles. While working at his father's John Deere dealership, Schlag began buying the parts from the local Chevrolet dealer's parts counter in the 1960s and stored them at the John Deere dealership. He also made annual trips to California, pulling a trailer behind an RV for a month at a time in order to retrieve

Fisette pressure-washed the cars he found from top to bottom and removed the interiors so they could be cleaned and thoroughly demoused.

About half of the engines Fisette found are big-block Chevrolets. The other half were small-blocks, but all were from factory performance cars.

Fisette chose to restore this 427-cid, 435-hp 1967 Corvette roadster, since he believes that was Schlag's intent with this particular car. The roadster's refurbishment will utilize new GM parts Fisette has found in the trailers, and by the time the car is done, "Everything under the car will be NOS," Fisette said.

more parts for his stash. When his father died and the dealership was liquidated in the early 1970s, Schlag tucked the parts and cars into semi trailers.

But when Schlag began to suspect the very people who he was saving parts for had betrayed him by stealing parts, he stopped sharing his collection. He even went so far as to completely seal the trailers once they were full. By butting up the trailers against each other, not even he could go back in them without some major effort. Schlag also stopped driving the cars he collected after one of his Corvettes was keyed in a parking lot. From that point on, he swapped the engines and slipped the

This shelving unit holds a small portion of the NOS Corvette parts uncovered.

Many of the cars hid rare parts in their trunks. This LS-6 1970 Chevelle SS454 carried Corvette knock-off wheels, a radio, parts for a fuel-injection unit, and several other items. A 1967 SS/RS Camaro carried three complete fuel-injection units.

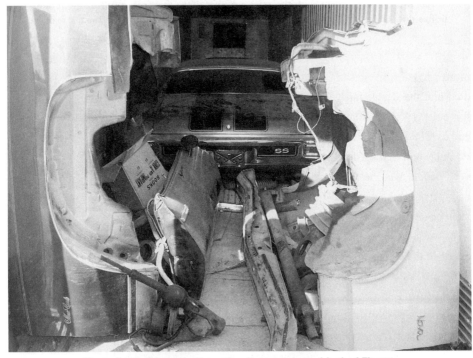

These front clips and other miscellaneous parts blocked Fisette from getting to the LS-6 Chevelles.

Corvette knock-off wheels are in demand, and Fisette uncovered a bunch. At least three full sets were part of the haul.

cars into the trailers, and that's where he left them.

Many local car collectors believe the reason Schlag pulled the engines from his cars and installed different engines before putting them away was to thwart thieves, since they wouldn't be numbers-matching cars. Even parts like a first-generation Corvette gas tank was separated from its two filler neck pieces, and its parts were spread among three trailers. Another theory was that Schlag knew the engines would be worth more than the cars, so he pulled out the hot engines and put slightly less desirable engines in their place.

Despite his unfortunate experiences with some of his fellow hobbyists, Schlag remained friendly. When scouring car shows

The trailers contained 125 steel Chevrolet engine crankshafts, five skids of M-22 and T-10 four-speed transmissions, 10 pallets of heads, and more than 150 engines.

and swap meets around Chicago, Milwaukee, and Green Bay for more parts in his rusty El Camino, Schlag could be herd engaged in conversations that sometimes eluded to his amazing stash.

"He'd talk about what he had, but he didn't brag and he didn't sell anything," said Fisette, who met Schlag on two occasions before Schlag's June, 2005, death. Through these brief interactions, people began to

Schlag is pictured in front of the trailers he used to store his collection of performance Chevrolet and Corvette cars and parts.

piece together what Schlag had been hiding.

And while no one knew exactly what Schlag owned, Schlag seemed to know what everyone else had in their garages. By being the local expert on fuel injection units and offering other mechanical services, Schlag became acquainted with cars in his area, which also helped him feed his collection.

"There was a rumor that Don would remove your big-block and install a small-block (as a gas-saving measure during the second fuel crisis)" Fisette said. This would explain why about half of the engines Fisette has uncovered are big-block Chevrolet engines.

When he learned Schlag had passed away, Fisette contacted Schlag's family.

"I called (Joanne Stepien, Schlag's sister), told her my name, and said I'd buy everything and told her I had the capability to disperse it all," Fisette said. After checking with other hobbyists, Schlag's family decided that Fisette was the right person to buy the collection.

"We were so lucky to find Larry," said Stepien. "I received several phone calls (from people interested in buying the collection), so I took their names and numbers. I had about five different people to choose from." Stepien then researched the reputations of each party, and Fisette was the only person to come back with stellar credentials.

Ever heard of a Davis big-block Chevy fuel injection unit? Well, here's a used prototype, and the mold to make more can be seen behind it. All Fisette knows is that Davis Engineering of Bellflower, Calif., produced the aftermarket unit using production small-block Chevrolet fuel-injection parts.

Once the deal was sealed, Fisette was ready to break down the doors of the trailers to see what he had bought. The first trailer he opened didn't let him down.

"I hadn't seen inside any of the trailers. I (bought) it all on Donny's reputation," Fisette said. "The first trailer I opened had two (1970 Chevelle) LS-6s in it," he said. "(My reaction) was absolutely total amazement." The Chevelles were parked bumper-to-bumper in the trailer, and the first he gazed upon was a gold, four-speed, bench-seat car that Fisette soon realized was the LS-6 Chevelle his neighbor had bought new. Fisette even

remembers the day the neighbor brought it home from the dealership and showed it to him.

Regardless of his memory of the car, Fisette prefers the Chevelle parked in front of the gold car: a blue Chevelle with bucket seats and an automatic transmission, which he considers more driveable.

Unearthing the Yenko Camaro shortly thereafter was obviously an exciting experience for Fisette, but opening a trailer full of factory performance engines made the hair stand up on the back of his neck.

"The most exciting moment was when I

This 1963 Corvette was a theft recovery car. A previous owner stripped the white paint before 1967 to reveal the fiber glass seams, which line the car like a butcher's chart.
(Steve Fisette/Tom Kujava photo)

opened up a trailer and saw shiny engines up one side and down the other, and then two stacked shelves of them," Fisette recalled. More than 150 high-performance engines have been found, in addition to 14 nice, low-mileage cars. However, the bulk of trailers contains parts... and lots of them.

Fisette organized the parts in a warehouse to best determine what he had. While looking down the line of engines, Fisette smiled at a complete engine for a 1969 Camaro Z/28 engine and asked, "Isn't that pretty? It's a DZ-302 that's complete down to the breather!" The Camaro 302-cid is

one of approximately six such engines he's found, and he's hopeful that it and many of the other engines will land back in the cars they originally came from, right down to the cast-iron 427-cid engine block for a COPO car he found in one trailer.

"I think (dispersing this collection) is going to give people a chance to make their cars correct," he said. One hobbyist has already contacted Fisette to ask if he has the original engine to his Nova, which was sold to Schlag many years ago following an engine transplant.

For Fisette, the hunt was more fun than

If anyone outside of an authorized Chevrolet parts counter deserved this sign, it was Donald Schlag, who collected the sportiest of sport-performance Chevrolet parts.

the catch, and he wants to share that experience with fellow car collectors. Pointing to a 1958 Corvette radio, he said, "Imagine how happy this is going to make somebody."

"I've done nothing but empty trailers since September," Fisette said while surrounded by all the parts he's organized in his warehouse. "I walk in here and feel like Scrooge McDuck. I can remember as a kid thinking, 'I'd kill for a four-speed.' Now look how many I have!"

Regardless of his few interactions with Schlag, Fisette feels he's come to understand the man. "I've really gotten to know (Schlag)through this puzzle," Fisette said.

Story update

Since the story ran, all of the cars and parts were sold to a collector in Maryland, who offered nearly all the treasures at auction. One 1970 Chevelle SS454 LS-6 from the collection is on permanent display at the AACA Museum in Hershey, Pa.

Story by Angelo Van Bogart
Photos by John Lyons

MANUAL-TRANSMISSION
CHRYSLER 300-G

**Only four manual-transmission Chrysler 300-Gs were known to exist until
John Lyons pulled this fifth example out of the weeds in upstate New York.**

Having one really rare car would be enough for most enthusiasts, but John Lyons believes in the adage, "the more the better." So when a manual-transmission Chrysler 300-G popped up for sale, Lyons jumped on the chance to add a second one to his garage.

"The moment I saw the ad, I called, trav-

"The moment I saw the ad, I called, traveled out to see the car, and bought it on the spot."

This code 281 300-G is also the only Cinnamon Metallic example Chrysler historians believe exists.

eled out to see the car, and bought it on the spot," Lyons said.

Of the estimated 40 or so 1961 Chrysler 300-Gs built with the code 281 three-speed manual transmission option, only four had been authenticated by experts. That is, until Lyons found this fifth code 281 manual-transmission 300-G on the internet. Since he's currently restoring a Mardi Gras Red 300-G with a manual transmission, he couldn't pass up the opportunity to score the long-hidden Cinnamon Metallic code 281 300-G.

The previously unknown 300-G hid from Chrysler 300 enthusiasts in a weedy nest in Stanfordville, New York, where it was parked for more than 30 years in the hands of the original owner's wife. Since the only option on the car is its manual transmission, some suspect its original owner intended to drive it a quarter mile at a time.

In 1960, Chrysler Corp. offered a French-built four-speed transmission, and according to some, the four-speeds were finicky, so a Chrysler-built three-speed manual was substituted in 1961. Currently, more 1960 Chrysler 300-Fs are known to exist with a manual transmission than au-

The floor-mounted shift handle can be seen just left of the console.

thenticated code 281 300-Gs, despite the fact more 1961 300-Gs are believed to have been built. This code 281 300-G is also the only Cinnamon Metallic example Chrysler historians believe exists.

The car is rough, but since its authenticity has been confirmed by the Chrysler 300 Club International, Inc., and it has been added to the short list of manual-transmission 300-Gs, the car is well worth the restoration effort.

At press time, Lyons reported that the Cinnamon Metallic 300-G had passed onto another 300 club member in good standing, and restoration of the rare 300-G is well underway.

FOUND: ONE-OWNER CHARGER R/T

Collector car dealership finds 9,800-mile Charger R/T four miles from its doors

A collector car dealership found this 9,800-mile Charger R/T four miles from its doors.

Bob Lichty, former *Old Cars Weekly* advertising manager, and his partner, Gary Brown, founded Motorcar Portfolio of Canton, Ohio, in 2003. Today, it markets more than 100 quality cars of all vintages.

The duo has been cautious to not get carried away with the hype of the muscle car boom, but they occasionally stock such cars. Otherwise, the business' focus is the tried-and-true collector and prewar antique and Classic cars.

"It does not seem that a day goes by, that

"It does not seem that a day goes by, that someone calls our store offering a car for sale."

someone calls our store offering a car for sale," Lichty said.

It was that very situation that netted the company an amazing find.

"Nine times out of 10, when a call offering a car comes in, it is something like a Valiant four-door sedan with a six-cylinder [and] automatic, or a rusty high-mileage luxury sedan needing more work than it is worth," Lichty said. However, one call from an area banker wanting to help a friend and client through a difficult estate dispersal proved to be the opposite.

The car in question is a 1969 Dodge Charger R/T. The car's data plate indicated it is a "Charger R/T special" with plain wheels, small hubcaps, redline tires, silver metallic paint, black "bumble bee" stripes and a bucket-seat interior. Best of all, it came with a 440-cid, four-barrel V-8 with a TorqueFlite automatic transmission.

The Charger was bought new by a man who recently died. And, it was only used for street racing on Friday nights and kept in a clean, dry garage from the start. The owner slightly modified the numbers-matching car by adding a three two-barrel Six Pack setup with a hot cam, headers, less-restrictive exhaust, Cragar gray-finish mag wheels

with Atlas Bucron tires and a Bell steering wheel. However, every item taken off the Charger was sitting on a work bench within reach of the car, right down to the complete original exhaust system.

By coincidence, the Charger was only four miles from the Motorcar Portfolio showroom. Ironically, Lichty, an old street racer from the late 1960s, would have cruised the same drive-in restaurants that this car frequented around the Akron, Ohio, area.

"It was like opening a time capsule," Lichty said. "The car was exactly what a person would have run on the street back in the day, right down to the Atlas tires sold at Sohio gas stations that had the best grip. A set of Atlas Bucron tires and a tank full of Sunoco 260, and you were ready for an evening of fun."

The car had only 9,800 original miles. It had its original upholstery, chrome and paint, right down to the R/T bumble-bee stripes. Workers at Motorcar Portfolio are slowly going over the car so its originality is not disturbed. Even a few minor dings have been left, as the car is detailed with preservation in mind. Lichty suspects the car would be a prime candidate for AACA

Historic Preservation of Original Features judging. However, the tires were dangerously dry rotted, and the company has since installed a set of correct bias-ply redline F-70x14 tires from Coker Tire to match the spare in the trunk, which has never been on the ground.

Motorcar Portfolio technicians also got the car running again. All the parts that were removed for the modifications were saved and will provide the next owner with the choice of returning the car to stock condition. However, they realize it may be just as attractive to keep the car as a time capsule of another era, when Friday nights were consumed with cruising drive-ins in a hopped-up muscle car.

By Angelo Van Bogart

ONE 'PLUM CRAZY' BARN FIND

One-owner 1970 Road Runner found 50 miles from new owner's home

After 33 years in the original owner's barn, this 1970 Road Runner recently saw the light of day when it found a new owner.

Larry Fechter of Iola, Wis., has wanted a 1970 Plymouth Road Runner from the time his big brother bought a new Lemon Twist (yellow) hardtop nearly 40 years ago.

"They have a 150-mph speedometer and we got close to pegging it," Fechter said. "It's the fastest I've ever gone in a muscle car."

That's saying something, because Fechter has restored many muscle cars through the years. His current stable includes a documented Daytona Yellow 1969 Camaro Rally Sport Z/28 nearing the end of a body-off-frame restoration, and a 1967 Pontiac GTO sport coupe wearing a very presentable older restoration. There's also a 1969

The original owner installed Keystone wheels and new tires immediately after buying the Road Runner, but kept the original Polyglas tires and steel wheels. Larry Fechter, the car's new owner, has reunited the car with the original wheels and tires.

Ford Mustang Boss 302 in his past and a 396-cid 1965 Impala convertible in his future, but memories of his brother's Road Runner never went away.

"I wanted a '70 — I didn't want any other year," Fechter said.

Less than 50 miles away, another Larry (we'll call him "Larry Smith") also wanted a 1970 Road Runner, and ordered a new Plum Crazy (purple) hardtop from Clark Motors, a Chrysler-Plymouth-Imperial dealer in Wisconsin Rapids, Wis. The 335-hp, 383-cid Road Runner was optioned with the Dust Trail Stripe, hood performance paint treatment, black vinyl top, fresh air pack carburetor (Air Grabber), light package, vinyl bucket seats and a solid-state AM radio. These options, plus the four-speed manual transmission and performance axle package (3.55, heavy-duty Sure-Grip 8-3/4 rear

axle), brought the final price to $3,934.55 after the destination charge. All told, the final price was quite a bump over the Road Runner's $3,034 base price.

After taking delivery, Smith immediately removed the original steel wheels, poverty caps and the F70x14 fiberglass-belted tires and put a new set of Keystone wheels on the Plymouth. Smith didn't care for the factory wheels, and planned to install aftermarket wheels well before he checked the first box on the order sheet.

"He didn't like the rims they had, so as soon as he got the car, he took the rims off and put the Keystones on it," Fechter said.

Smith also immediately mounted a Sun tachometer and a statute of Jesus Christ to the top of the instrument panel.

"[Smith] dated his wife in the car and installed red lights under the seat with a

After a thorough cleaning, the Road Runner's original interior looks new. That hole in the floor will soon host the original Pistol-Grip shifter again. A "Road Runner" emblem has been added to the instrument panel.

switch for when they parked," Fechter said.

All of that cruising and parking was done in the summer months. Wisconsin weather can be brutal, and the salt used on the roads can be devastating to sheet metal, but this Road Runner never saw the street in

Aside from perhaps plugs and wires, you can bet the parts on this 335-hp, 383-cid V-8 are date-coded. The motor pulled the Road Runner for 55,000 miles before it developed an oil leak and was removed from the car and left untouched.

the winter. But even with all that care, the Plum Crazy Road Runner's 383 developed an oil leak after six years and 55,000 miles and was pulled from the road.

"In '76, the car had a rear main oil seal leak, so he pulled the engine out and never got to it," Fechter said. At that time, the transmission was also removed and the car was placed in a barn.

The meeting of two Larrys

Even though the two Larrys were less than 50 miles apart and shared an interest in '70 Road Runners, they didn't meet until late 2008, when Larry Smith had a friend list his Road Runner for sale on a local Web site. Larry Fechter was the first to spot the ad.

"I was working in the shop on a Satur-

According to factory manuals, the Air Grabber "cool-air inlet system takes air through vacuum-operated, hood-mounted air scoop and directs it to the carburetor air cleaner." A driver control could also open and close the scoop.

day, took a break and went in the house," Fechter said. While looking on the Internet, Fechter stumbled onto the Road Runner and called the phone number and left a message. Like the Coyote chasing the Road Runner, Fechter left another message on Sunday, even though the ad had been pulled from the Web site. The Road Runner could run from Fechter, but it couldn't hide.

It took until Monday evening for Fechter's phone to ring. On the other end was the person who listed the car for Smith. Apparently, the seller had been deluged with calls and pulled the advertisement after four hours. Smith knew interest in the car was high, but since Fechter was the first to call, he was offered the first chance to see the car.

"Someone had offered them [more than] the asking price," Fechter said, "but the person in charge of selling it had integrity and honesty and said, 'You have first dibs.'"

But the chase wasn't over. Fechter had to wait until the following Friday to see the car, and since interest was strong, he wasn't sure the deal would go through.

"With these things, you don't even talk about them with other people until they're settled," he said.

When Friday arrived, Fechter and his

"It's one of those things you dream about. To find a car like that is like getting hit by lightning — it only happens once."

wife, Rhonda, had their cash in hand, but it was hard to tell if the Road Runner was worth the chase.

"It was so dusty, you couldn't even tell what color the vinyl top was," he said. Fechter determined that underneath the dust gathered from years of barn storage was a solid, one-owner car that wouldn't be hard to get back on the road again. On top of that, the car came with all of the right documentation, and like other muscle car collectors, Fechter appreciates a car with proven provenance.

"It's unbelievable what documentation he had," Fechter said while holding the original window sticker. In addition to paperwork, the car also included an original bottle of partially used Plum Crazy touch-up paint and an extra set of Dust Trail Stripes. Since the car arrived with a defect in the stripes, the dealer had included a new set with the car. Smith never applied them, and they remain in the original blue-and-white MoPar boxes.

"I couldn't believe I found it, and one with a four-speed, Air Grabber [hood] and

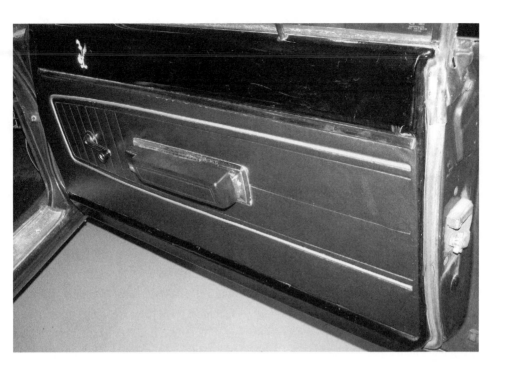

High Impact Paint," Fechter said. "It's one of those things you dream about. To find a car like that is like getting hit by lightning — it only happens once."

Knowing the price was not negotiable, Fechter looked over the car with its engine and transmission parked nearby and contemplated its value. Smith said he'd throw in a set of manifolds and carburetors removed from an old street racer's Chrysler engine to seal the deal, and Fechter finally had caught his Road Runner.

"It wasn't easy for Larry to sell it," Fechter said. "When we saw the car, his wife was gone, and after I said, 'I'll take it — here's the cash,' his wife came back. She started crying because they dated in it."

The Road Runner meets its second owner

Fechter wasn't prepared to haul the car, so after completing the deal, he returned home with original parts that Smith had removed from the car when the engine was pulled. Smith had kept track of all the removed parts, including the long-handle Hurst Pistol-Grip shift handle, barely used original wheels and tires and other bits. Fechter loaded those parts, as well as the odd intake manifolds and carburetors from another MoPar, took them home and returned Saturday for the car. That day, the dusty Road Runner slowly rolled into the sun's rays for the first time in more than three decades, courtesy of an Oliver tractor

"I don't call it a two-owner car, I call it a 'Two-Larry car.'"

employed to pull it from the barn.

Once he got the car home, Fechter sprayed off the years of dust from the exterior and engine compartment. He also cleaned the cobwebs and dust from the black vinyl interior and found it to be in like-new condition. Likewise, the vinyl top quickly returned to its as-new luster. Fechter removed the back seat and found two build sheets that confirmed everything in the paperwork he already received on the St. Louis-built car. The glove compartment revealed more documents of the car's history, such as period road maps and a registration sheet.

To check the electrical system, a battery was hooked up and all of the headlamps lit up; even those bulbs under the seat emitted a red glow again.

Now that the car is cleaned up, Fechter isn't sure what to do with it. Should it be restored? Should the engine and transmission be cleaned up and returned to their place otherwise untouched?

"I want to solicit ideas from people what to do as far as restoration," Fechter said. "You don't want to devalue it [by restoring a good original.]" Noting its overall good,

solid condition, he noted, "It's a good problem to have."

In the meantime, Fechter is doing his research before he tears into any part of the car, a process he expects will take about two years.

"I'm going to gather as much information as I can," he said.

Some of that information may come from the original owner, whom Fechter remains in contact with. After cleaning the car, Fechter took photos to document it and included one photo at the end with a 12-pack of beer on the roof. He sent it to Smith and told him the beer and car would be waiting for him if he ever wants to visit.

"I don't call it a two-owner car, I call it a 'Two-Larry car,'" Fechter said.

And what about those odd intake manifolds and carburetors from the street racer that Smith threw in with the deal? They're rare and desirable 1961 Chrysler 300-G long-ram manifolds, valuable in and of themselves. Not a bad bonus in a deal that already included a new friend and a great car.

Story and photos by Angelo Van Bogart

FOUND! STASH OF CORVETTES IN ORIGINAL OWNER'S HANDS

After being disappointed by the trade-in offer for his 1969 Corvette while buying a new 1975 'Vette, Walter Hacker decided to keep the '69; he also decided to go ahead and buy the 1975. The cycle continued until he owned four Corvettes, but with an offer from muscle car hunter Larry Fisette, Hacker decided to sell all of the 'Vettes to make some garage space. Here, the Corvettes are being removed from Hacker's garage.

Some guys have all the luck, but Larry Fisette of De Pere, Wis., says he isn't one of them. For Fisette, finding desirable cars is more than luck — it's a skill acquired through hard work applied to building connections and a reputation as a car hunter.

Fisette, owner of De Pere Auto Center, is best known for his huge muscle car and Corvette find that included 21 trailers filled with high-performance Chevrolet parts and cars, among which a Yenko Camaro, LS-6 Chevelles, and fuel-injected Corvettes were counted. A more recent find wasn't quite as large, but it was still very impressive.

For what is probably the first time in its history, this 1,500-mile 25th Anniversary Corvette felt a few raindrops as Fisette was picking it up. While preparing it for sale, he found the original build sheet still clinging to the top of the rear axle. Had this car seen more miles, the build sheet would certainly have been a goner.

Thanks to a lead from an employee, Fisette found four low-mileage Corvettes in the hands of their original owner, and only seven miles from his business. The Corvettes were discovered while the employee was at a garage sale and noticed a partially disassembled red 1975 Corvette parked on jack stands down the street. He told Fisette about the car, and when Fisette went to investigate, he learned the Corvette's owner had three more Corvettes stashed in his two-car garage. It also turns out the sheltered Corvettes were even more desirable

cars, and were in better condition.

In the garage, the owner, who made a living as a baker, had a 9,800-mile 1969 Corvette with a 300-hp 350-cid engine. Next to it was a 25th anniversary 1978 Corvette with 1,500 miles and all of its stickers on the windows, including the dealer tag on the windshield. The third Corvette in the garage was a 1985 with 7,000 miles on its odometer.

The owner said that after selling his 1963 split-window Corvette for a more family orientated car, he yearned for another Cor-

The trade-in ritual became a trend for Hacker, and before he knew it, he was sitting on four Corvettes.

vette, so he picked up the 1969 when it was new. When he decided he wanted a new Corvette in 1975, he learned the bad part of the new-car trade-in business.

"They wouldn't give me nothing for it, [even though] it didn't have any miles on it," Walter Hacker said. Disappointed by the trade-in offer, but determined to buy a new Corvette, Hacker decided to keep the 1969 'Vette and buy the 1975. The trade-in ritual became a trend for Hacker, and

before he knew it, he was sitting on four Corvettes.

Despite their low mileage, the Hackers got their use out of them. The 1975 found in the driveway has recorded 45,000 miles, as it was used by Hacker's wife as her daily driver for several years.

"They're fun cars and we did enjoy them," Hacker said. "We went to Elkhart Lake [Wisconsin] and Bloomington Gold with them."

"I just love the thrill of the hunt."

Three of the four Corvettes were squeezed into Hacker's two-car garage, including this 9,800-mile '69 Corvette with a 300-hp 350-cid. This was the second Corvette Hacker purchased, and he learned from the sale of his 1963 to never sell again.

When Fisette approached them, Hacker's wife became excited about the prospect of regaining some garage space. Fisette explained that, in addition to his restoration business, he also enjoys tracking down forgotten cars and putting them back into the hobby. After a deal was struck, Hacker agreed to sell the cars to Fisette, who cleaned them up and put them on the market.

"I just love the thrill of the hunt," said Fisette.

By Angelo Van Bogart

THE ULTIMATE GARAGE ART: NOS BILLBOARDS

To photograph the massive billboards, which hover around the 9-ft.-high-by-20-ft.-long mark, Randy Littlefield uses a ceiling-mounted camera with a wide-angle lens. This 8-1/2 x 19-1/2-foot Veedol sign is priced at $2,200. (Randy Littlefield photo)

Remember whistling down a desolate stretch of two-lane highway at night in your 1949 Buick? You may have reached down to adjust the radio tuner in order to hear Sinatra's latest hit clearly through the chrome grille speaker cover on your dashboard while watching the nighttime scenery. If you were lucky, you might have spotted an illuminated sign advertising the new 1955 Chevrolet and its futuristic Panoramic windshield, or a set of red-and-white Burma-Shave signs lining the road like candy canes on a Christmas tree. Those days are gone.

Today's highways are hedged with signs declaring the benefits of a certain company's insurance coverage, or the location of an upcoming fast food restaurant. You many even spot an ad for the new Kia or the latest minivan. But roadside signage used to be a bit more interesting, at least for old car lovers.

Now you can take a part of the roadside past you miss so much into your home or garage with your own Richfield oil, Oldsmobile, Nash, or war bonds billboard, thanks to Randy and Sharon Littlefield and their expansive selection of new-old-stock bill-

The ultimate piece of artwork for any 1954 Chevrolet owner or lover with the space to display it is this 8-ft.-by-19-1/2-ft. billboard that shows a Bel Air Sport Coupe in front of a dealership. The sign is near the top of the price scale at $2,600. (Randy Littlefield photo)

board signs. As fascinating as the items in their collection is the story about how they acquired the roadside advertisements.

"I was never really interested in billboards 'til I acquired them," Randy Littlefield said. "While we were living in Meridian, Idaho, in 1981, we heard there were some billboard signs for sale through an antique dealer friend of ours in eastern Oregon."

The couple went to the dealer's shop and looked at a folded-up sample sign, but they couldn't get a good idea of how the picture on the billboards would look when they were laid out. But they were intrigued and wanted to learn more about the signs. The dealer explained that the signs were for sale, because there were being stored in a potato cellar in eastern Oregon, and the owner of the building wanted to bulldoze the cellar.

It's a good thing that the Littlefields were interested in the signs, because the cellar owner didn't realize their value. He had already given away several 1960s billboards to someone who was going to use them as insulation in a mountain cabin.

A couple of months after their first visit, the Littlefields went back to the antique dealer's shop and took a few of the new, folded-up billboards home with them for a closer look. The Littlefields soon learned many of the billboards are about 8-1/2 feet tall and 19-1/2 feet wide. One of the couple's friends told the couple how neat they thought the signs were, and not long after that the Littlefields decided they needed to make a pilgrimage to the cellar for a closer look at the sign stash.

"I decided right then that I wanted to check them out in person," Randy said. "The next day, I drove over to the potato cellar. The building was about 150 feet long and

Setting up a billboard

Laying out larger-than-life-size art can be quite a challenge, but the Littlefields have set up enough that they have a system.

The unused billboards weigh 5 lbs. and arrive unassembled and folded in eight to 16 pieces. The Littlefields recommend laying the pieces on a floor so that the design can be viewed in its entirety.

Since the pieces have been folded for as many as 60 years, the Littlefields hold down each section and flatten it with weights on top of thin boards. For wrinkled sections, the couple has found that an iron-rite press will steam the wrinkles out well. When the sign is flat, the pieces are ready to be assembled.

Each piece overlaps another in marked places, and it is in these places where the sign's pieces can be connected with a roll-on glue.

After the billboard is glued together, medium-weight cardboard can be used to support the back of the sign. For the front, the Littlefields recommend using 1-in.-by-2-in. lumber to frame the perimeter of the sign; this makes it easier to hang on a wall, yet it isn't permanent. To store the signs rolled up, a PVC pipe that is as long as a billboard's height can be used.

some 50 feet wide with a dirt roof. It was dark and had a musty odor throughout, and there was farm machinery stored inside."

Dust covered everything, including the huge stack of ads. Only the ads stacked on the bottom were damaged by mildew, but, unfortunately, they were the oldest ads. Randy and Sharon found the price of the stack to be reasonable, and began loading them into his truck for storage.

"As I moved these billboards into storage, I read some of the descriptions on the side panels of some: Santa Claus — Coca Cola (1947), Levi's, Signal Gas, 1955 Chevy, Bob Hope, and War Bonds. I really felt like I had gone back in time as I stacked the billboards into storage," Randy said.

The ads stayed in storage through a move from Idaho to Oregon, then had to wait until the Littlefields could get shelving that could support the weight of the 1,000-plus folded signs before they could be closely examined.

"What a thrill opening each one up. It was like opening up a time capsule." And they're still not done going through the ads. Some of the colorful and still-sealed billboards remain in their post office-metered packaging and date as far back as 1944.

Movie stars and celebrity singers appear in many of the ads, particularly the "bathtub" Mercury advertisements from 1950, and rank among the most desirable and expensive billboards the Littlefields sell. Jack Benny is pictured with a red Mercury sedan

This 1949 Packard billboard advertises the company's low-priced leader at $2,224, as delivered from the factory. (Randy Littlefield photo)

Brilliant colors and great art earn this beautiful 9 x 19-1/2-ft. Richfield sign a $2,500 price tag. (Randy Littlefield photo)

with the slogan, "Pinch-penny as Benny!" and Jane Wyman is shown with a blue 1950 Mercury convertible on a sign that reads, "A winner like Wyman."

Other billboards depict a profile view of a 1953 Studebaker two-door hardtop, a Chrysler Hemi engine, or a Henry J. There is also a wide selection of 1957 Chevrolet car and truck billboards from the "See the U.S.A. in your Chevrolet" era, as well as Chevron, Mobile, Shell, and Texaco billboards from the 1940s to the late 1960s.

The Littlefields are also car collectors, so they kept a Packard billboard to complement their collection of Packards and a 1949 De Soto convertible billboard to go along with

The 1954 Nash Rambler club sedan was offered at $1,550 when delivered new from the factory. Fifty-five years later, a billboard featuring the car will cost more than that! (Randy Littlefield photo)

Buying a billboard

Looking for the ultimate garage art? Then a billboard might be your answer. If you find the sign of your dreams or the perfect complement to your car or petroliana collection on Billboards of the Past's web site, here are some things you should know.

The signs, in general, are 9 ft. tall by 19 ft. long, and are printed on specially treated paper that the Littlefields say is easy to work with and fairly heavy. Usually, each billboard comes in eight to 16 separate pieces that are folded up.

Prices for each billboard are determined by the type of artwork on them and the desirability of the item advertised. As such, prices vary from $50 to $3,000. Automobile advertisements that picture cars are usually priced from $2,200, but others featuring a company's emblem and motto can be found starting at only a few hundred dollars. At the top of the scale are ads that include celebrities and full car views, like the 1950 Mercury billboards.

To view an online catalog of billboards, go to www.billboardsofthepast.com. Orders can be placed through the web site, or by writing to: 5654 S.E. King Road, Milwaukie, OR 97222. The Littlefields can also be reached at 503-659-0266 or billboardsofthepast@comcast.net.

Muscle car lovers would ache for the space to show this 1967 Camaro SS billboard, and they'd need a lot of it, as it occupies 9-1/2 x 21-1/2 ft. (Randy Littlefield photo)

their similar 1948 model. A World War II-era Richfield oil billboard featuring planes and tanks was also set aside for their personal collection.

The couple has been selling the remainder of their thousands of billboards through swap meets on the West Coast. Sales are also completed through their web site, www.billboardsofthepast.com, which in itself is a virtual museum showcasing more than 1,000 pictures of their sold and unsold billboard inventory. Several museums, movie studios, restaurants, antique collectors, and car hobbyists call themselves customers to

the Littlefields' business. Recently, a yellow 1956 Cadillac Sedan deVille billboard was sold to General Motors for use in its museum, and among the several that have been sold to movie studios was a Navy billboard that can be seen in the movie "Men of Honor."

Other billboards can also be seen in person at the Nostalgia Antique Mall in Gresham, Oregon, or, if you're lucky, you might spot one at a restaurant or antique mall on the West Coast. And if you've got the space, you can see one of your own each time you pull that 1949 Buick into your garage.